Splashes
OF PINK IN MY LIFE

Embrace Your Quirkiness and Live Life to Its Fullest

Ravindran Amudha Jaishree

This book is dedicated to my nephew.

First published by Ultimate World Publishing 2023
Copyright © 2023 Jaishree Ravindran

ISBN

Paperback: 978-1-922828-91-0
Ebook: 978-1-922828-92-7

Jaishree Ravindran has asserted her rights under the Copyright, Designs and Patents Act 1988 to be identified as the author of this work. The information in this book is based on the author's experiences and opinions. The publisher specifically disclaims responsibility for any adverse consequences which may result from use of the information contained herein. Permission to use information has been sought by the author. Any breaches will be rectified in further editions of the book.

All rights reserved. No part of this publication may be reproduced, stored in or introduced into a retrieval system, or transmitted in any form, or by any means (electronic, mechanical, photocopying, recording or otherwise) without the prior written permission of the author. Any person who does any unauthorised act in relation to this publication may be liable to criminal prosecution and civil claims for damages. Enquiries should be made through the publisher.

Cover design: Ultimate World Publishing
Layout and typesetting: Ultimate World Publishing
Editor: Alex Floyd-Douglass
Photographer: Ken Wong – Back Cover Image

Ultimate World Publishing
Diamond Creek,
Victoria Australia 3089
www.writeabook.com.au

Contents

Foreword	1
Preface	3
Chapter One: Lactoferrin	7
Chapter Two: Vipassana	13
Chapter Three: Fontana Di Trevi, The Wishing Well	27
Chapter Four: How Do I Know I Am Living My Life Fully?	37
Chapter Five: Jai'Z Anjarai Petti	45
Chapter Six: Sexy Life Lessons and Pearls of Wisdom	59
Chapter Seven: Discovering Seven Principles with Ella	71
Chapter Eight: Searching for Infinity	79
Chapter Nine: Universal Truth	97
Chapter Ten: The Journey to PhD	129
Chapter Eleven: Collection of Poems	141
The Games We Played As Kids	191
Recommended Books	203
Acknowledgements	205
About the Author	207
Speaker Bio	209

Foreword

"If you are lucky enough to meet Jaishree Ravindran in your daily life, I can guarantee that her distinctive soul-print will get fire-stamped on you and it'll remain there for long, like it happened to me years ago.

I meant to simply get a breakfast in a small town by myself and ended up having an amazing conversation that extended for hours and that magically convoked many more to the table. She is so brutally transparent that can be seen at a very first sight, she is curious, and she cares about you, so don't be scared about all her questions, she wants to know you more and find common ground to connect, discuss and most importantly to learn with joy.

Jaishree is a juvenile spirit that underwent deep self-exploration along resolving real life situations, sometimes with joy and laugh, sometimes with tears. This first book is an initial conversation sharing life learning experiences, anecdotes, advices and stories of everyday challenges gathered during the young adult life of a passionate woman, who you are about to meet."

Dr Cristian Moreno García

Preface

Why am I even writing this book?

To become famous? Leave a legacy? Or to share knowledge or all of the above?

I ask these questions often. I also feel I do not have much time on planet earth and want to make the most of what I can offer, experience, and share.

It has taken me over 41 years to really hone this and concentrate where I find tears of joy and sadness at the same time.

Sometimes I feel I want people to know me… Really know me. Not the *oberflecke* (on the surface) version but the real me.

The motivation behind me writing this book was that I wanted to be responsible and focus on the 'integrity' aspect of *"I will do as I say and say I will do."*

I strongly believe that each one of us is a living legend, some shine their light on others, some on themselves and some shy away from it all.

Splashes of Pink in My Life

I have been a combination of all at various times.

If you meet me for the first time, I'll give you my best energy as long as I have had a good sleep, good food (hot and savoury), and it is pleasant weather.

I like to live with a purpose – I ask myself how can I be purposeful to the situation I am in? Even at weddings, events, or crowds, I think about how I can help or be useful in this situation.

The only time I relax is when I am asleep. Yes, I like to go to bed early – unless it is a karaoke or a deep dive into soul searching talks or hitting the dance floor with my favourite music, of course!

I was born in India in a state called Tamil Nadu. I was in India until the age of 15 where, just 15 days after my 15th birthday we moved to New Zealand. The land of long white clouds: Aotearoa.

After couple of years at school in New Zealand, I represented the country as an AFS Scholar – an international cultural exchange student in Switzerland. On my return from Switzerland, I completed my tertiary education – Bachelor of Technology in Food Technology and Master of Dairy Science and Technology. Thus, I started my career in the dairy industry.

Fast forward few years and I have been immersed in a high value dairy protein called lactoferrin. Having worked in the field for over nine years, today I am doing higher degree by research in this sparkly pink protein. Yes, I am a PhD student.

Preface

Today, I am considered as a subject matter expert in lactoferrin. I remember once hearing someone say that at a lactoferrin conference and I shied away at the time, not sure if I believed in myself.

So, how should you read this book?

I invite you to read any chapter at any time, in particular order. If you are like me and like to reflect, then read a chapter, reflect and I am sure you shall find what you are seeking for in your life – be it peace, joy, happiness, love, solution, or grace.

The first way to open the gates of opportunities is to be aware, acknowledge, act, and get out of your own way!

All the best and I invite you to connect with me as we create, implement, and progress in our lives.

So grab a pen and get ready to explore and discover the Splashes of Pink in YOUR life.

Chapter One

Lactoferrin

This chapter is dedicated to the lactoferrin manufacturers I have worked for as a Technologist; Murray Goulburn (now Saputo), Synlait, and Bega Cheese.

I am truly grateful for the experiences, challenges, and the space to grow both personally and professionally.

One thing you will learn about me in this book is that I really enjoy writing poems and often comes as an answer to a question that is seeking a way to express itself. I wrote this one dedicated to my work in the field:

Morning dawn and in the evening dusk
Lactoferrin spread like mystical musk
Iron bound valuable protein
Ion exchange lactoferrin
Bloody red in elution
Purity seeking solution
Playing purity versus yield
A game to capture in the field

Apo (lactoferrin) is free of iron
Mono is only with one iron
Holo is saturated with iron

Several shades of salmon pink
Precious and costly just like mink
Nutraceuticals uses and in infant milk

Crazy about this sparkly pink
Discover them on my eyes as I wink
Right from head to toe do you see the link?
How many shades of pink
Did you find as you blink?

Time for some pink reflections...

1. What did you get out of this chapter?

   _____

   _____

   _____

   _____

   _____

2. What came to your heart, mind and body as you read this chapter?

   _____

   _____

   _____

   _____

   _____

3. What resonated with you?

_____

_____

_____

_____

_____

4. What would you like to share?

_____

_____

_____

_____

_____

_____

5. What is your take home message?

_____

_____

_____

_____

_____

_____

Chapter Two

Vipassana

I heard about Vipassana through two people. The first, a traveller from Germany I met at Oamaru Backpackers in New Zealand.

All I recall was, she said she sat and did yoga every day in her room. I imagined her sitting cross legged on her bed in a dorm and doing her own thing where at times, she probably fell asleep. She was travelling with a small glass jar where she kept her waste. I had heard about it on YouTube – how to live a zero-waste life. I remember thinking, good for her!

I also heard about Vipassana through Cris, I call him Salsa Cris – we met at Hanmer Springs Salsa Festival in July in New Zealand. The moment Cris mentioned Vipassana I knew I wanted to do it, too. It felt like a deep calling as I heard about it from him.

While at Vipassana, I had completed 10 hours of meditation a day for 10 days – that is a total of one hundred hours of meditation!

Prior to learning about Vipassana, I was meditating for 21 or 31 minutes a day as soon as I woke up. I liked it. I felt elated and thought, hmmm, this will keep me going.

The question then arises, what is meditation?

Is meditation really just vertical sleeping?

What is the difference between sleep and meditation?

What could have prepared me for Vipassana?

When I told my work colleagues about Vipassana, they were so nervous – how can one be without talking for ten days?

My work mates and friends could not believe I could be without talking for ten minutes, let alone ten days!

I had my own prejudices about meditation. I held a little bit of fear that it would change me into something or someone else.

When I told Karren about my silent retreat, she suggested I write down the answers to three questions before the retreat and rewrite the answers after the retreat.

1. What do you want in life, Jaishree?
2. What is important to you in life?
3. What are the top three problems in your life, Jaishree?

I kept thinking and pondering about these three questions.

I had flown from Miami to Los Angeles and to Auckland, New Zealand. And when I was on the way to the retreat, I remembered, I better answer the three questions Karren had asked me before the retreat. I finally wrote the answers down as the taxi pulled into the Vipassana Centre.

So, the first question:

What do I want in life?

The answer was simple, clear, and straight forward.

No questions or second thoughts… I wanted a Noble Prize!

I don't know what it is about the Noble Prize, I just knew I wanted one. I also pondered if I wanted a relationship, a loving partner, a companion in life or was it too much hassle? I left it aside.

Vipassana

Next up was the question:

What is important to me in life?

This took a while to answer. One of the answers to this question is and was hygiene. When I went on a road trip with my work colleagues – who became good friends – it irked me going to the toilets in the National Parks and not having a soap to wash my hands with.

Since I was driving on our road trip, I always had a mini toiletry stash in my car – in case I need to stay the night at friend's house, or got stuck in the middle somewhere. I had a body wash, extra toothbrush and paste, extra underwear, tissues and an extra pair of clothes.

I often referred to the kit as the 'boyfriend kit', in case I met someone… and had to spend the night. I love to be prepared.

The basics of personal hygiene was to help me feel clean and hygienic, no matter where I was. The answer took me by surprise and yet, I was also not surprised. Liquid soap to wash my hands! This was just before the pandemic where the use of hand wash and sanitiser became big in 2020!

I quickly scribbled the answers on my iPhone as I was heading to the retreat – cleanliness, my parents, friends, brother, simplicity, wealth, travels, passion, zest for life, and love. In no particular order and all very important to me.

When Karren asked me about question three, I said, *"I see challenges not problems."*

Splashes of Pink in My Life

She replied, *"Don't give me that!"*

The thing is that I genuinely see challenges not problems and my mind went into a flashback, taking me back to my childhood.

When I was young, I would get so excited about challenges I had in life, I didn't see them as problems. I would sit and analyse, talk, think about them until I had a breakthrough.

These challenges were like hidden opportunities and treasures and when there were no problems, it would make me sad as if I felt like I had nothing to solve.

At times when I was told, *"Here comes trouble,"* I would add the words, *"Yes, trouble-shooter!"*

I enjoyed facing problems/challenges head on – be it people, situations, or things. I would not let go until I solved them.

This included confronting people and having a difficult conversation. It saddened me when I found people had issues or concerns with me and didn't talk to me directly. I understand now why that might have been the case and fully acknowledge them.

I recently finished listening to an audiobook called *Help-Me* by Marianne Power. I could see glimpses of me – could very well relate to that book too – be it in relationships, being a nice, polite, kind person, seeking validation, or getting interested in guys who are not interested in me and vice versa.

I liked her style of writing; her way of social experimenting.

Vipassana

I decided to look up the dictionary for the word 'problem' and its true meaning. Here is what the dictionary tells us:

According to the Oxford Dictionary online, problem is a thing that is difficult to deal with or to understand; a question that can be answered by using logical thought or mathematics.

> *Word origin for 'problem'*
> *Late Middle English (originally denoting a riddle or a question for academic discussion): from Old French probleme, via Latin from Greek problēma, from proballein 'put forth,' from pro 'before' + ballein 'to throw'*

Challenge means a new or difficult task that tests somebody's ability and skill, an invitation or a suggestion to somebody that they should enter a competition, fight, etc.

> *Word origin for 'challenge'*
> *Middle English (in the senses 'accusation' and 'accuse'): from Old French chalenge (noun), chalenger (verb), from Latin calumnia calumny', calumniari 'slander'.*

> (https://www.oxfordlearnersdictionaries.com) site visited September 2022

Through Vipassana, I understood and experienced that if you are aware and equanimous, you have conquered yourself, your mind, your life. Anything! Manifestation is powerful.

I want to write this book and publish it as soon as possible.

I want to keep up with my sharp focus and clarity in life.

Splashes of Pink in My Life

So, what is this Vipassana all about?

I started talking to my colleagues about this; they were very intrigued. And initially, I was hesitant thinking, I should pen this down for my book – keep it original with pure thoughts.

And soon I realised, the more I talked about it, the more structure I got. I got better at telling people about Vipassana… Some were amazed, some joked, some laughed, and some wanted to take it up.

I felt as if I was an ambassador for Vipassana. It reminded me of one of the stories that was told on the discourse night. When a guy asked Buddha, *"Why do you tell everyone about this knowledge?"*

To which Buddha replied with a question, *"Do people ask you about your village where you come from and does every person you say go to visit your village?"*

The guy responded, *"No."*

Buddha smiled and concluded, *"Some will go, some don't. It doesn't matter."*

Vipassana means 'to see as they are.'

Practising Vipassana, I realised to see as they are means without any preconceived notions, any judgements, and actually seeing and experiencing as life is.

In Vipassana, meditation involves concentration on the body and its sensations, and the insight which this provides.

The first three days at the retreat were focusing on *aana-paana* meditation. Focusing on your breathing, no changes, just observing how the breath goes in and out of the nostrils – and slowly moves into gradually feeling the sensations around the nose.

Out of the 100 hours, the first 30 percent is focusing on the breath. The fourth day onwards goes into the Vipassana technique – feeling the sensation form top of your head to your feet – chunk by chunk and then sweep en masse.

To experience this is to really experience the reality what is happening within you.

It is an experiential truth that I faced. Lot of things came to the surface – one of them was writing a book, another one was Cris who told me about this meditation, and thirdly about work. How could I solve this technical problem at work?

Time slowed, and everything around me slowed, especially the meditation hours. I could not fall asleep, I was restless and looking forward to finishing up. I wanted to run away and run as fast as possible! Although restless, I kept my eyes closed until I heard the gong!

My mind thought a lot about Cris, about work, about my book writing, and PhD. I was mad at Cris for telling me about Vipassana and that I was suffering. I thought had he not told me I would not be doing this. I imagined us meeting up and telling him about how it was for me and how I was swearing at him and feeling sorry for myself.

I was getting angry and mad at myself for not keeping up with my promise of publishing my memoir. I was feeling like a failure.

Splashes of Pink in My Life

All sorts of emotions came up and I silently cried behind those closed eyes. I even thought about my PhD.

Maybe I should just find a solution to the lactoperoxidase and go do a PhD, travel the world, write a book, and live a simple life. Just make sure I had enough undies to get me through two weeks without washing.

Something shifted, maybe it was the discourse, maybe it was the food, maybe it was that focus on myself that I had longed for. I could pay attention to others but never really paid attention to what was happening inside me – my feelings, emotions and then there were the sensations.

I knew and had experienced that when I have an issue or grudge with someone that it was not them, it was me. I had been working on this for a very long time and could see how your outer world is a reflection of your inner world.

There were three things that kept coming up as cravings. It went on until day six where, when I look back, I feel it was from day seven onwards that I had my breakthrough.

Only recently, I weighed myself I noticed I had lost weight. It was not intentional, but it happened. I went back to the weight I always wanted. It was effortless.

So according to the teachings, we either have aversions or cravings. And how do you conquer your mind and overcome these aversions or cravings? Each aversion and craving create what is called as *shankara* (impressions). In Sanskrit, shankara is known as *samskara*.

*Saṅkhāra (**Pali**;* सङ्खार; ***Sanskrit***: संस्कार *or saṃskāra)* is a term figuring prominently in Buddhism. The word means 'formations' or 'that which has been put together'. Being aware of our breath, our sensation and responding rather than reacting has become the theme of my new life.

I got more than I bargained for. I went with an intention that I wanted clarity, I wanted more awareness. I got much more than that. I not only learnt about meditation, I learnt what was true liberation.

I also learnt that spiritual growth is measured through equanimity of the mind. I realised I did not crave and think about food so much. I realised I got what I wanted even if it was oil for my hair or soup for the evening without any feverishness. I really learnt how to relax. I learnt how to be self-determined and not beat myself up about all the small things.

I also learnt that I had to and wanted to keep up with my practises and it's okay if I miss out.

Now time for some deep reflection...

1. What did you get out of this chapter?

   _____

   _____

   _____

   _____

   _____

2. What came to your heart, mind and body as you read this chapter?

   _____

   _____

   _____

   _____

   _____

3. What resonated with you?

_____

_____

_____

_____

_____

4. What would you like to share?

_____

_____

_____

_____

_____

5. What is your take home message?

_____

_____

_____

_____

_____

_____

Chapter Three

Fontana Di Trevi, The Wishing Well

This is a story about a time when I was loving and living my life and career like none other. This is a chapter from my life when I was on a high-flying disc to a place where I was so low. I recollected, gathered myself wondering how this impossible and improbable thing happened to me?

Where, how, and why did it all go to custard?

I loved the place I was living in. I fell in love as soon as I saw the backyard; a luscious green secret garden. The backyard had dense trees on the outskirts of the fence giving a feel of as if I was in a secret forest. The room overlooked the garden – trees with beautiful green leaves and yellow flowers reminded me of the gold and green – a beautiful combination just like my cousin's saree.

I managed to negotiate the price and moved in end of the month. It was beginning of spring; the bus stop was close by and the house was nestled and located in a prime location.

I loved the kitchen and I could get back into my cooking. I enjoy cooking – if it is gas stove, it is a bonus! I got smart and was efficient to pack the essentials in a box due to various moves and I had it all ready.

I had a job I loved that I was very passionate about and looked forward to going to work every morning. I often colour co-ordinated my outfit.

My flatmate was a lovely, young, energetic and sporty lady who loved horror movies, especially crime scene investigation, and Home and Away. Although we did not spend a lot of time with one another, each of us was busy with our own things.

I was at the peak of my career, enjoying life and meeting people. I had the opportunity to go to a conference in Rome – yes, it was the lactoferrin conference!

Rome out of all the places. It was like a dream come true.

I love packing my holidays tights… and being on the go go go.

My host mom had told me about Fontana di Trevi in Rome – make a wish and drop a coin. So, when I was in Rome for six hours during a mini backpacker holiday in 2011, I toured the Colosseum, then the Palatino, and during lunch break, I dashed off to Fontana di Trevi to make my wish.

Five years later, my wish came true. Yes absolutely! There was a Lactoferrin conference, and it was happening in Rome!

How amazing is that?

I loved and lived for my work – so much so that my clothing correlated to the product lactoferrin that I worked and believed in so much. Sparkly pink and just fabulous with its magical properties! Anti-fungal and anti-bacterial, it's a magic wonder protein that is found in milk. It is in extremely low quantity in milk that you have to process millions of litres of milk to extract hundred kilos of the powder.

In another context, one gram can be found if you were to consume 20 litres of milk. You get the picture. And now I was going to Rome for the Lactoferrin conference. I was going to be immersed in the product, and with the world experts, meeting so many delegates from all over the world – scientists,

Fontana Di Trevi, The Wishing Well

business developers, students, lecturers, professors, many other manufacturers and the list goes on!

Finally, when I landed in Rome, I was chauffeur driven to my hotel where the conference was held. The driver waited with my name on a placard 'Jaishree Ravindran' and it was a Mercedes limousine. I was living my dream, flying high and was in Rome on an official business trip.

This time before I went to Fontana di Trevi, I was happy and grateful for the one wish that I had made had come true. I ran, thanked and said a sincere prayer of thanks when I visited the Trevi fountain. I took coins from my colleagues to drop in the fountain on their behalf – I was a postie (postman) for the Trevi Fountain.

I was a mere carrier of the coins and later as time went by, I found out all their wishes had come true!

I was so fascinated with Fontana di Trevi, I said my prayers and thanks and added, *"Dear Trevi Fountain, I am thankful to you for making my wish come true – my official business trip to Rome. Last time I made a wish and it was the only wish, and it came true after five years. Could you make this one come faster, please!"*

This time, I wished to see a good friend from another part of the world by chance and to let the universe surprise me.

I dropped the coin and completely let go. Not many people knew that I was travelling to Rome for work. I was having a fabulous time enjoying gelato, visiting the pasta shops, checking out souvenir shops with Pinocchio, and since it was close to Christmas, I also got several presents for my near and dear ones.

Splashes of Pink in My Life

There was a designer shop with Italian leather shoes, jackets, and hand bags... Michelangelo!

I went into the shop and was browsing in the shop. I bought a green and red bolero. The green bolero would match my green Doc Martin's shoes and the red one would be elegant when wearing evening gowns or dresses. It was going to be my birthday on the conference dinner night, too. A celebratory outfit indeed!

It must have been under a couple of hours since I had made the wish. As I walked out of the store, I was astonished at who I saw – a good friend, all the way from Melbourne, Australia. Yup, Bala! Neither Bala knew I was in Rome nor I knew Bala was in Rome.

When we met in Melbourne in passing, we mentioned, *"Oh wouldn't it be nice to meet in Europe sometime?!"*

The minute, I saw Bala, I was baffled, awe struck and told Bala and my friends about the wish I had made literally a few hours before.

This is a photo of Bala and I outside the shop.

Fontana Di Trevi, The Wishing Well

Bala and I in Rome, Italy

Bala was visiting another town in Italy from Australia and stopped over in Rome for a brief visit.

Bala along with my friends, we enjoyed a nice Italian pasta for a lazy lunch and after lunch we parted ways.

Later I learnt why the wishes of Fontana di Trevi come true. Apparently, the holy waters reach Vatican City. I do not know if that is the case, but it would not surprise me as the hydro-engineering in Rome is simply amazing.

Yes, it's that time for deep reflection...

1. What did you get out of this chapter?

   _____

   _____

   _____

   _____

   _____

2. What came to your heart, mind and body as you read this chapter?

   _____

   _____

   _____

   _____

   _____

Fontana Di Trevi, The Wishing Well

3. What resonated with you?

_____
_____
_____
_____
_____

4. What would you like to share?

_____
_____
_____
_____
_____

5. What is your take home message?

_____

_____

_____

_____

_____

_____

Chapter Four

How Do I Know I Am Living My Life Fully?

I often wondered and asked this question, and the answer came to me in a form of a poem when I was travelling between Melbourne and Leongatha, back in 2010. I penned it down, so that I would refer to this anytime in my life.

How do I know I am living my life fully?

When you are in the pink of health is when you know you are living your life fully!

When I am concerned and not buried in worries
Yet handle situations gracefully without any hurries
When I am contended with myself and no stress
Yet patiently make slow and steady progress
When I don't compare myself with others
Yet be inspired like beautiful peacock feathers
When I am ready to have fun, explore and learn
Yet be very satisfied with what I earn
When I understand and befriend my mind
Yet with all I grow in love and bind
When I am able, serene, peaceful and absolutely cool
Yet clearly express without letting my emotions rule
When I realise temporariness of worldly pleasure
Yet continue for that ultimate precious treasure
When I have a smile with or without comfort
Yet be kind and useful without any effort
When I communicate and touch the heart of all
Yet let not the physical distance matter at all
When I glance and catch a glimpse through the eyes
Yet spoken silences of deep meaning and unfathomable ties
When I close my eyes and stretch my back to relax
Yet stay alert like slow burning candle wax
When I feel modest and humble for my achievements

Splashes of Pink in My Life

Yet be disciplined in routine and daily managements
When I am amazed and appreciate nature and art
Yet be able to decode the science completely apart
When I can build on the intelligence
Yet sustain curiosity and innocence
When I understand we are all one consciousness
Yet individually have infinite means of complete goodness
When I can discriminate between good and bad
Yet be indifferent to people's past that they have had
When I realise I can create heaven on earth
Yet indulge in emptiness and its birth
When I am focused at work I become one
Yet be playful, enjoy, and have lots of fun
When I am in discussions and have differences of opinion
Yet be harmonious and be a great companion
When I am sure and confident without a doubt
Yet unknown of the outcome before time is out
When I am equanimous in word, thought, and action
Yet speaking from the heart without any hesitation
When I am bemused by life's purpose and my role
Yet put all effort towards the set goal

... When I work whole heartedly
... When I feel 'extra' ordinary
... When I know I am not in a hurry
... When I have no regrets nor am I sorry
... I know I am living a life ... happy and peacefully!

How Do I Know I Am Living My Life Fully?

It's that time again. Let's take a moment for some insightful reflection...

1. What did you get out of this chapter?

   _____

   _____

   _____

   _____

   _____

2. What came to your heart, mind, and body as you read this chapter?

   _____

   _____

   _____

   _____

Splashes of Pink in My Life

3. What resonated with you?

_____

_____

_____

_____

_____

4. What would you like to share?

_____

_____

_____

_____

_____

_____

How Do I Know I Am Living My Life Fully?

5. What is your take home message?

_____

_____

_____

_____

_____

_____

Chapter Five

Jai'Z Anjarai Petti

I have had interest in food from a very young age. I am grateful to my mother, along with the many women, and the men who have inspired me to do anything related to food and cooking. My grandma, paternal and maternal aunties and relatives and so many more have given me recipes and will be sharing the best ones here – including a simple guide to my spice box – my Anjarai Petti.

Anjarai Petti means spice box in Tamil. Pronounced *unji* in Tamil means five, *arai* means compartments and if you are in for a bit of pun, *arai* can also means 'slap'!

I was given Anjarai Petti many years ago and still treasure it – it's a very important tool kit. I have an extra Anjarai Petti that I have still kept it unpacked, perhaps to be gifted or I may use it myself one day.

Each Indian household will most likely have one in stainless steel or plastic with a different spice combination. I have shared my Anjarai Petti with more than five compartments.

Splashes of Pink in My Life

Jai'Z Anjarai Petti - the centre one is turmeric, there is chana dal (kadala paruppu), urad dal, mustard seeds, cumin seeds, fennel seeds, and dry red chillies.

This is a classic Anjarai Petti for tempering, also known as *tadka* in Hindi or *thalikuruthuku* in Tamil.

The purpose of this chapter is to share my favourite and key recipes with you. These are also shared on my recipe planner/placard for beginners or for those who want to be efficient with their time.

Jai'Z Anjarai Petti

Key: O = Optional, D = Diced, S = Sliced

Gravies and side dishes	Seeds			1T	Paste		Fresh			Powders				Other			Variations
	Mustard	Cumin	Fennel	Onion	Ginger	Garlic	Onion	Tomato	Green chillies	Turmeric	Chilli	Coriander	Cumin	Cloves	Cardamom	Cinnamon	
1. OT Curry	✓		✓	D			D	✓	✓	✓	✓						Add grated carrots
2. Avva's Kurma	O	✓	✓	S	✓	✓	✓	✓	✓						✓		Vege/chicken; Make a paste when cooked with cashew/almonds, white poppy seeds, coconut powder
3. Mimmee's Chicken Fry		✓			✓	✓	✓			✓	✓	✓					Drumstick
4. Meena Athai Aloo Palak		✓			✓		✓				✓		✓				Add potatoes/paneer/peas
5. Yoghurt curry		✓			✓				✓	✓			✓				Okra/Zucchini/Lotus root
6. Bombay Aloo	✓					C			✓	✓	✓		✓				Peas optional
7. Amazing Aloo fry	✓	✓								✓	✓	✓	✓				
8. Pooja Cauliflower	✓	✓								✓	✓	✓	✓				
9. Egg OT Curry			O	✓			✓	✓	O	✓	✓						Good with roti or wraps
10. Avva's muttai (egg) fry							D	✓	O								Make a paste in oil and fry
11. Egg bhurjee (scrambled)		✓				✓	✓	✓	✓				✓				
12. Peas curry/dip			✓							✓	✓						
13. Cabbage Fry	✓		✓		✓	✓	✓			✓	✓	✓	✓				Peas and cinnamon - optional
14. Yara (Prawn) fry	✓		✓		✓	✓	✓	✓		✓	✓	✓	✓				
15. Meena Mushroom Fry		✓	✓							✓	✓	✓	✓				Fennel powder

Fast fifteen from Jai'Z Anjarai Petti

Key
- O = Optional
- D = Diced
- S = Sliced
- P = Powder
- L = Leaves
- BC = Black cardamom

Key
- C = canned
- SK = Soaked

	Seeds			1T	Paste		Fresh				Powders				Other	Additional			Instructions
	Mustard	Cumin	Fennel	Onion	Ginger	Garlic	Curry leaves	Onion	Tomato	Green chillies	Turmeric	Chilli	Coriander	Cumin	2 Cloves / 2 Cardamom / 1 inch Cinnamon stick	Cashew nuts	Mango powder	Fenugreek leaves/powder	
Rice																			
Coconut Rice	✓	✓	✓	✓	✓	✓		S		✓						✓			Have this with chicken fry / Add coconut milk/powder
Tomato Rice	✓	✓	✓	✓	✓	✓		S	✓	✓	✓	✓				✓			
Jeera Rice		✓		✓		✓		✓		✓						✓			Have this with chicken fry
Peas Pulao		✓			✓	✓		D								✓			Good combo for Kurma
Quick lentils																			
Mung beans (whole)[SK]		✓			✓	✓	✓	D			✓	✓	✓	O	O, BC		O		Good combo for Kurma
Chick peas[C]	✓	O		S	✓	✓	✓	✓	✓	O	✓	✓	✓	✓	✓, BC		✓	O	Add sweet potato
Black eyed beans[SK]	✓	✓		✓	✓	✓	✓	✓	✓	✓	✓	✓	O	✓	O, BC		✓		Add potatoes
Red Kidney beans[C]	✓			✓	✓	✓	✓	✓	O	✓	✓	✓	O	✓	✓, BC		✓	O	Add potatoes / soya chunks

Variety Rice & Quick Lentils from Jai'Z Anjarai Petti

Jai'Z Anjarai Petti

Welcome to Jai'Z Anjarai Petti

Avva's kurma (20 - 45 minutes)

- In mortar and pestle make a paste of
  - Paste 1 - cloves, cardamom, cinnamon, ginger, garlic, cumin seeds, fennel seeds, chillies
  - Paste 2 - poppy seeds, coconut powder, nuts (cashew/almond)
- Heat wok, add oil, add cumin and fennel seeds, add bay leaf.
- Add sliced onion (1T), then add Paste 1. Simmer and add remaining onion, let it sauté for 5 minutes, add salt.
- Add veges/chicken, add powders (turmeric, chilli and coriander and then tomatoes
- When cooked add Paste 2, let it cook (boils and thickens)
- Add coriander leaves to garnish and ready to enjoy!

Thair Pachadi (Yoghurt salad)

1. Yoghurt
2. Cucumber
3. Carrot
4. Black salt (optional)
5. Amchur (mango powder)
6. Cumin powder
7. Chilli (optional)

Mix yoghurt with other ingredients (sliced / diced - your choice)

Pious Payasam

- Semiya / tapioca
- Milk
- Sugar/Jaggery
- Cardamom
- Cashew nuts and sultanas/raisings

Fry semiya/tapioca in ghee/butter along with nuts, add milk and cardamom. When all ingredients are cooked, add sugar

M&M - Meena Mushroom Fry

1. Chop mushroom in halves
2. In a hot wok / kadai add oil, when ready add mustard seeds
3. Add powders - turmeric, chilli, coriander, cumin, and fennel
4. Add salt to taste
5. Garnish with freshly chopped coriander

Doll Kadayal

1. Wash lentils (moong and masoor)
2. Dip in water, add asafoetida, turmeric, garlic cloves, chilli, salt, tomato, turmeric, few drops of oil
3. Optional veges - zucchini, eggplant
4. After two whistles in pressure cooker - blend
5. Temper with dry chillies, mustard seeds, curry leaves
6. Garnish with freshly chopped coriander

Chapati / Roti

1. Make soft dough with wholemeal/plain flour
2. Add salt, yoghurt, ajwain (optional) to flour and make soft dough
3. Make a circle, add oil and fold into half, add oil on the quarter and fold again to form a triangle
4. Evenly roll pin to give a triangular shape
5. Different shapes lead to different layering
6. Stuff it with potatoes or veges for parathas

Simple Rasam

1. Tomatoes, garlic, coriander (include stalks), curry leaves, cumin seeds
2. Soak tamarind in hot water for ten minutes
3. Add coriander powder
4. Mix all contents, add salt to taste and cook
5. Temper with - mustard seeds, dry chilli, asafoetida

Condiments

1. Mixed vegetable pickle
2. Pappad - microwave 3 pappad for 50 seconds and flip
3. Cook for another 10 seconds if required
4. Yoghurt drink - blend yoghurt, fresh ginger, chillies, and coriander leaves and blend with a pinch of salt

Rice

1. Soak rice - 1 to 2 hours prior to cooking
2. Temper with cumin seeds, bay leaves, and cloves
3. Add soaked rice and cook

Would you like to learn more?

Call Jaishree on +61 4774 19271
Email Jaishree.SplashesofPink@gmail.com

Nine Gems from Jai'Z Anjarai Petti

I had the unique opportunity to run a couple of cooking workshops in Tatura Community House and this is the flyer and recipes we used.

An Indian Food Journey – Tatura Flyer from Community Event

I am extremely grateful to my mother, father and the support from the Tatura Community to make this dream come true.

After a lot of planning and discussions with my mother, we came up with nine recipes – right from starters through to dessert as shown in *'Nine Gems from Jai'Z Anjarai Petti'*!

In Indian cooking, it is a very different experience. There is no set way to eat such as starters, mains, and desserts – especially in the south, where the food is served on a banana leaf.

When you go to a South Indian wedding, the first thing that is placed is a savoury dish, followed by sweets, like *kesari* or *laddoo*, then several curries (fried vegetables), then rice, then sambar (liquid lentils).

After sambar is yoghurt, and then we finish the meal with *rasam* also known as pepper tamarind water to aid digestion.

The way I have implemented this in my life is I like to start the relationship sweet and when inviting friends and family over for lunch or dinner, I start by serving a sweet dish. It is entirely up to them when they choose to have it.

So, at this workshop, I was able to share my knowledge and experiences about Indian culture I was brought up in. I was brought to happy tears (later on after the event) as I was so amazed that no matter who did the cooking, especially the kurmas – even the participant who had never cooked Indian food – it was exactly the same as if my grandma had prepared it in her kitchen!

I felt her grace and her blessings and have tears in my eyes as I write this!

Ingredients for Avva's Kurma

Splashes of Pink in My Life

Delicious dishes from the Workshop at Tatura Community House

I also want to share key recipes that I use as remedies for health.

For gastro or food poisoning, I prep the following:

- Dry fry about one teaspoon of cumin in a wok on low heat.
- When the seeds start to pop, keep shaking the wok - toasting and tossing.
- When the popping slows down, add a cup of water and let the concoction boil for five minutes.
- When the water is brownish in colour, simmer and filter the drink.
- For sweetness, you can add a teaspoon of honey when the liquid is warm.

This is my go-to remedy for recovering from flu/gastro/food poisoning. I have the concentrated form when I have fever. I do not take the concentrated form more than twice a day. Or I have the diluted form, in one to two litres of water as liquid intake for the day.

Good luck and speedy recovery!

For colds and sore throat, I take a pinch of *ajwain* with warm water. For immediate relief on sore throat or cold, I take two to three peppercorns and bite once and sip a glass of warm water.

For relief from a runny nose, I grate fresh ginger and add a dash of honey with few drops of lemon, followed by warm water. I have the ginger concoction three times a day at the first sign of a runny nose. And for hay fever or nose congestion, my go-to health supplement is Blackmores Horseradish Garlic + Vitamin C.

Time for some delicious reflection...

1. What did you get out of this chapter?

   _____

   _____

   _____

   _____

   _____

2. What came to your heart, mind and body as you read this chapter?

   _____

   _____

   _____

   _____

   _____

3. What resonated with you?

_____

_____

_____

_____

_____

4. What would you like to share?

_____

_____

_____

_____

_____

5. What is your take home message?

_____

_____

_____

_____

_____

_____

Chapter Six

Sexy Life Lessons and Pearls of Wisdom

The Sexy Lingerie Theory

I came up with this theory many years ago... and it is so true! Personally, wearing lingerie is sexier than turning up naked because...

Something hidden, something revealed
Overall enticing and mysteries sealed
Break the code
Fashion in mode
It is a concoction theory
I call it the sexy lingerie theory!

This is what makes any person attractive, charming, and why you feel the desire to be in their presence.

It is this feeling of naughty and nice!

Pearls of Wisdom with Rishi Vidyadharji

Thanks to personal development and inner soul searching, I got to spend valuable time with Rishi Vidhyadharji from Art of Living. Rishijis in India are spiritual leaders and revered as holy men.

Here are summaries from the learnings of timeless wisdom:

Four ways to handle the mind:
1. Faith – things will change.
2. Somethings do not change – so what, just accept it.
3. Wake up the valour invoke – take the challenge, take the plunge.
4. Offer it to the divine – helplessness through prayer.

Four types of problems faced by humans:
1. Negative emotions – anger, sorrow, regrets, jealousy, etc.
2. Boredom – wanting for new.
3. Inertia – disinterest in life.
4. Mistrust – inability to let walls down.

There are four ways to encourage or entice the mind:
1. Fear
2. Reward
3. Love
4. Discipline

Identify where do the problems lie – the root cause – and apply the solutions.

Ever since I came across this knowledge, I have been able to transform and apply these pearls of wisdom and transcend the problems.

Problems in life are due to an excess or too much of love. Have you heard the story of Ramayana?

Ramayana is a famous epic. An epic of a prince who was sent on exile. The ancient epic is about his life while on exile and how he rescued his wife with the help of monkeys.

Rishiji summarised the nectar as Hanuman is for breath, Ram the soul, Sita the mind, Lakshmana the awareness, and Ravana the ego.

The story goes like this. Lord Rama was on an exile with his wife Sita and brother Lakshmana. His wife Sita was abducted by Ravana when she crossed the boundary drawn by Lakshman for her protection. Hanuman helped in the search for Sita.

The philosophy of Ramayana was boiled to when the mind (Sita) steps beyond the boundaries of awareness, the mind is overtaken by the ego (Ravan) and the mind is separated from the soul. Both the mind and soul become sad. Through breath (Hanuman), the mind and soul are united back together.

Rishiji talked about lessons from Ramayana at the spiritual retreat. I took lots of notes and was reluctant to share. When I reflect, I do not know why or if there was a reason for not sharing.

Applying Rishiji's wisdom here and sharing the knowledge – knowledge when shared is only multiplied.

Ram the Soul (Self)
Sita the Mind
Ravana the Ego
Lakshmana the Awareness
Hanuman the Breath

When the mind steps outside awareness, it is overtaken by the ego, leaving the soul to become *dukhi (sad)*.

The 10 Heads of Ravana:

When loving each of the following more than required, it manifests into a feeling:

1. When we love status, that becomes ego.
2. When we love somebody too much this is attachment.

3. Having expectation of perfection and wanting that from others translates to anger.
4. Expecting oneself to be perfect leads to guilt and sorrow.
5. Loving one's past and comparing the past too much leads to regret and hatred in the present moment.
6. Too much love for the future can lead to fear and anxiety.
7. Excess love for an object or things leads to greed.
8. Loving one's appearance and vanity in excess leads to jealousy.
9. Love for too much fantasy in excess leads to lust.
10. Loving security in excess leads to inertia.

This is also known as the 10 heads of Ravana. Ram is known as a symbol for commitment. Ravana was destroyed by Ram.

When we observe these negative emotions, they transform into positive energy. When we observe, we are aware and with awareness we can respond rather than react to the situation at hand.

Universal truth has no discrimination on skin colour, bank balance, age, sex, or country.

Very much linked to the first law of Thermodynamics, *"Energy can neither be created nor destroyed, it can only be transformed from one to the other."*

When we observe a sensation in our body, the sensation transforms, depending on how long we have observed it objectively.

When we watch our breath during meditation, we have a lot of thoughts and when we observe them without judgement – just like watching television – we become aware where we can respond, rather than react!

A few more pearls of wisdom that I acquired spending time with Rishi Vidyadharji:

- Wanting to be with a person is attachment
- Not wanting to be with a person is detachment
- Using a person is lust
- Being useful to a person is love
- Bringing out the divine in a person is devotion
- Love gets fragrance with devotion
- Hurry and worry make a man diseased
- Impatience and intolerance cause problems in life
- Looking for love results in loneliness
- Looking for respect results in insult
- Looking for perfection brings anger

Four things in life change – feelings, emotions, judgements, and logic. Only knowledge is constant.

When learning from any situation, the knowledge should be positive.

I spent quite a bit of time with Rishiji and noticed this on his bag: *"Know breath, know life."*

When there is no breath there is no life! I experienced various patterns in breathing when I was sad, happy, angry, hungry, or focused. There are a lot of secrets in our breath.

Life is this experiment and we are the subject and also the subject matter experts of our own breath.

Rishiji also imparted the knowledge that the seven chakras have instruments associated with them. For example, when there is inertia (the chakra related to base of the spine) and lethargy, we transform, or our energy gets transformed with the drum instrument.

The belly – often related to jealousy – has the same sensation as when we experience 'butterflies' in our tummy. That's why the laughing Buddha has a big belly!

The heart chakra is associated with string instruments.. That's why you see a cupid with a violin. If you are watching TV and you hear the violin, I invite you to mute and keep watching.

Do you still have the same effect or are you affected? That's why perhaps the guys would serenade with a guitar to declare love for their beloved.

The throat chakra is associated with gratitude and sorrow.

When we feel sad, our throat chokes and the same sensations are observed when we feel gratitude. The instrument associated with the throat is flute – hollow and empty.

The one above the throat is the head chakra, where the sensations are related with anger and awareness. Have you ever seen someone so focused, their eyebrows frown and they appear very serious and/or angry?

I have experienced this many times where I've been focusing so hard that I have a very serious face and look as though I am angry. The instrument associated with this are the bells. So, when we enter a temple, we ring the bell – we become present to the place of worship.

When I was in Switzerland, my host mother would ring the bell, and it meant dinner is ready. If it was rung out of meal times, it meant drop everything you are doing, and come quickly – we need to meet for something very important. It meant time to be alert.

Every chakra has two sides and gets transformed from negative to positive when we observe it. The only one that is not two (Advait) is about six inches above our head also known as the crown chakra and the feeling of bliss.

The instrument associated with this is the conch shell. Perhaps that's why in temple, the conch is blown to activate the bliss that is deep, dormant or active within us.

And perhaps that's why in funerals there is the drums and the conch – to bid good bye to the body.

I also find these two key points of wisdom that keep me going on the earthworm story that I heard from Ken. I call him Yoda as he's full of wisdom!

Ken said, *"Jaishree, it is easy to look at the dirt when we dig soil but to look for earthworms, you've got to look closer. Another way of looking at this is asking oneself, what is going right and has been going right?"*

This helps me focus on the goodness, rather than dwell on the faults.

Time for some deep reflection...

1. What did you get out of this chapter?

   _____

   _____

   _____

   _____

   _____

2. What came to your heart, mind, and body as you read this chapter?

   _____

   _____

   _____

   _____

   _____

3. What resonated with you?

_____
_____
_____
_____
_____

4. What would you like to share?

_____
_____
_____
_____
_____

Splashes of Pink in My Life

5. What is your take home message?

_____

_____

_____

_____

_____

_____

Chapter Seven

Discovering Seven Principles with Ella

I looked forward to teaching and coaching Ella. A wonderful and very dedicated diligent student. Ella was shy and quite reserved. Her mom Nicki was very driven, and I could see a beautiful bond of a mother-daughter relationship. Often it reminded me of my mother, how she was so invested in what I learnt at school.

Every Sunday, I would go to Ella's house and start the coaching session by asking how does she feel? And how does she rate her maths?

It set the pace. I learnt about what made her tick, what excites her, and what she likes. My main aim and motivation were to weave these excitements into the things she didn't find so exciting i.e., maths.

Each week, I gave Ella tasks and I was amazed at how she was very dedicated and diligently finished them all. I also learnt what her strengths were and the areas she did not like. I would explain to Ella a couple of methods to do the same problem and let her choose what resonated best with her.

As months went by, I felt I was gathering and solidifying my knowledge which was universal and could be applied to any aspect of life.

Such principles when composited came to the following seven principles:

1. Time my maths. Find out how long it takes to solve the problem. Embrace the current situation wholeheartedly with full acceptance, and no judgements. Be willing to take the steps for improvements without being harsh on myself.

2. Identify the problem. My father often says, *"Define the problem"* as a problem well defined, is a problem half solved.

3. Methods and processes. What methods or processes are available for me to use?

4. Evaluating the methods. Which method is most suitable for me? This could be based on experience, on intuition, on comfort – essentially the path of least resistance.

5. Practice, patience, and persistence. Have faith that this will get me somewhere. Believe and have the confidence things will work out.

6. Progress – with practice, speed increases, confidence builds, and patterns evolve.

7. Energise – when tired, run down, or upset, find something that makes you smile. In Ella's case, I asked her to think of horses. Personally, for me, it's writing, cooking, dancing, cleaning, talking, and planning. Planning gives me a sense of perfection and vision of what I like and what I look forward to.

I so enjoyed coaching Ella that I lost myself… I felt zoned out, worry-free, and had a great sense of purpose. At times, it felt like being in a trance but completely aware and grounded to the problems at hand – ready to solve. I loved coaching because it helped me discover and reemphasise my beliefs and key principles where I felt free to apply them in my own life.

Discovering Seven Principles with Ella

With Ella in New Zealand

Thank you, Ella and Nicki!

Time for some more deep reflection...

1. What did you get out of this chapter?

   _____

   _____

   _____

   _____

   _____

2. What came to your heart, mind, and body as you read this chapter?

   _____

   _____

   _____

   _____

   _____

3. What resonated with you?

_____

_____

_____

_____

_____

4. What would you like to share?

_____

_____

_____

_____

_____

Splashes of Pink in My Life

5. What is your take home message?

_____

_____

_____

_____

_____

_____

Chapter Eight

Searching for Infinity

How did this chapter get revealed?

I joined the Ultimate 48 Hour Author Workshop and one of the participants was sharing that their book was going to be about job search. I resonated immediately and wanted to share my story – searching for infinity within and without.

Within

Within is referring to the inside world – life wisdom, knowledge, experiences, and reflection.

My search for infinity was through holy men in robes, holy books and asking questions about enlightenment.

When I saw Rishi Vidhadharji, I asked what is Nirvana also known as enlightenment?

And he gave me an instant demonstration. I loved it and the wisdom he imparted! He asked to hold my arm straight and to hold a 500ml water bottle. Rishiji asked me to hold it for another minute.

Then he asked me, *"Is the bottle getting heavier?"*

I responded, *"Yes, it is!"*

As the time kept increasing, the bottle felt heavier and heavier. Although it was the same volume and mass of water, it felt heavier and heavier over time.

After many minutes passed, he asked me to leave the water bottle and told me that, *"The feeling of letting go is Nirvana! That is what we do with life, we hold on to things — physical and emotional so much that it gets heavier and heavier in our hearts that we are compressed by our own miseries."*

A twist to this story was when I was in New Zealand and thought this was my great way to teach people about Nirvana, a young scientist, I lovingly called her Patanjali, opened my eyes.

She said I would hold on to the bottle in such a way it is not a burden and I feel comforted and provided comfort.

This was revolutionary for me to mention that, *"Wow, I can have and hold the bottle without any pain!"*

Rishiji often said that money when shared is halved. If you have $42, when shared between two people, each gets $21. When shared amongst three people, it becomes $14. The more you share the less each one gets.

In the case of knowledge, when you share it doubles. Now you know the story and I know the story. And if each one tells another ten people, the knowledge/story multiplies by ten or many folds!

Another story that I would like to share here about infinity is an experiential one.

I was in Bali for a Teacher Training Retreat for three weeks through The Art of Living. One of the days, I was late for my yoga session in the morning. I was asked to wait outside, in the lobby. I was standing there and doing my asanas in the lobby, while the other participants were inside following the instructions.

I was fascinated by the reflection. As I looked to my left – there was a mirror and my reflection. I looked to my right – there was another mirror and my reflection. And as I looked closer and deeper, I realised there were reflections of the reflections, reflections of the mirror on both the sides.

I was blown away by the magnitude and that's when it dawned on me. Often when I have met people, they are a reflection of myself, my deepest soul, and although they may appear different from the outside, it is my experiences that shape my world.

So, there are infinite reflections that we come across in life who are our deepest reflection is some shape or form. Be it in the form of a teacher, a friend, family, or even people we judge or have strong opinions about in our lives.

A good friend once said, *"It is often the things that we do not like in ourselves that we do not like in others."*

And often we forget the first part and have strong opinions about others. I have also come across in life, where I have the utmost admiration for a person, only to discover that I had that trait within me. So not just the negatives, it is also the positive qualities and attributes that we eventually find within ourselves and feel humble about them.

Another way where I have found infinity is through dancing. One of the forms of classical Indian dance is Bharatnatyam. I am very grateful to my dance teacher Jayashree Nair, founder and director of Upaasana Akademy of Fine Arts, Mumbai – www.upaasana.com

I am in awe to see three generations – Jayashree Teacher, Sujatha (her daughter) and Sharanya (her granddaughter) come through the academy. I feel extremely blessed to have reconnected with Jayashree Teacher when my friend Pooja expressed interest to learn Bharatnatyam.

I learnt Bharatnatyam as a child from fourth standard (aged nine) to tenth standard (aged 15) and although I did not complete my Arangetram, I often could imagine the dance in my mind whenever I heard classical music or any music to which I could dance to.

I felt transported to another ethereal level where it was bliss and expression of a divine art form. Teacher has often spoken about there being no difference between the dance and the dancer and I have often experienced this when practising and also when listening to Carnatic music. In my high school days, I learnt this classical form of dance for six years from Jayashree Teacher. And after moving to New Zealand, I would often revise and perform in small groups – *alaripu*, a classical piece that means offering to the Divine.

After almost 27 years, I am continuing to learn Bahratnatyam online from Jayashree Teacher. Thanks to Pooja and her interest to learn the dance form that it has given me the opportunity to reconnect to this classical fine art.

I find Pooja's love for dancing very addictive and I have been able to rejuvenate my long-lost passion. Thank you Pooja, let us keep dancing away under the tutelage of our beloved dance teacher – Smt. Jayashree Nair. I hope and pray that we shall perform our *Arangetram* on stage one day.

Three generations of Upaasana Dancers

Searching for Infinity with the Outer World

Without is referring to the outside world. The outer world consisting of that which we can see touch and experience with our five senses, i.e., the physical world.

Once we have discovered there are infinite possibilities within ourselves, we can search for infinite possibilities with the outer world. Having a purpose, a career, mission in our lives are a sense of security that we seek and want in our lives. It could be for various reasons – constant income, a status, sense of purpose, sense of belonging, and each one may have a different answer why do we want security and assurance in our lives.

We often seek this security through work for a constant income; a certainty that we can take care of ourselves, our loved ones, our commitments, our family, friends, or even a greater purpose.

When we were in New Zealand, every Saturday our family – yes, my parents, brother and I – would discuss the career section from the Saturday newspaper. It was an activity that I reminisce now and enjoyed at that time. My father collected the clippings for several years while we were at school and continued this right through our tertiary education.

We would discuss it at great lengths and practise the questions very relevant to our lives. For example, the CEO of a company would be asked, *"What makes your day? Tell me about yourself. What was the most challenging decision in your life and how did you overcome it?"*

These are great reflective questions and I often answered how they were relevant to my life, with examples that were current. I once went for an interview where I was asked, *"Tell me about yourself,"* to which I responded, *"What would you like to know?"*

Do you think I got the summer placement in the company? No way! After an interview, I often reflect on my questions and answers with my parents.

Here are the golden nuggets of wisdom that I acquired over the years of my life and feel these are very applicable even today. Yes, even for cold calling and networking.

Prior to applying for a new role/job:

Make three key contacts with the company.

1. First contact – get to know more about the role and express your interest and let them know you will be applying for the role. Speak to the relevant manager and/or human resources in the company.

2. Second contact – call and let them know you have applied for the role.
3. Third contact – let them know you are visiting the area and would love to catch up. By putting a face to the name, you have already done three points of contact.

Most likely they will contact you for an interview.

I would like to elaborate that in between the point of first and second contact – your resume and cover letter need to be well thought out. I have used this format and it has worked very well for me. The name of the file as 'First Name, Last Name for Position' e.g., 'Jaishree Ravindran for Lactoferrin Technologist'.

Additionally, the resume must have your phone number and email on one side – preferable the right-hand side and that states: 'Resume current as of XYZ date'.

An example of my resume is shown below.

Splashes of Pink in My Life

Jaishree Ravindran

Email Jaishree.Ravindran@gmail.com
Phone +61 4774 19271

Personal Profile
I believe in personal and professional development. My long-term ambition is to grow and develop with the industry needs and to advance my expertise in science and technology.

Jan 2019 – June 2022
Bega Cheese – Technologist – Bionutrients
- Subject matter expert for Bionutrients' products and processes
- Coordinate trials and project management to deliver outcome

October 2018 – Jan 2019
Jai Creations – Dairy Technologist
- Technical Services for the food and dairy industry in Australia and New Zealand

June 2015 – September 2018
Synlait Milk Ltd – Lactoferrin Development Technologist
- Provide technical expertise on products, processes, and ingredients
- Technical reports, specifications are kept up to date as requested by Technical, Regulatory, Quality and Operations Teams
- Participate and work on specifications for product specifications, testing frequencies, Certificate of Analysis, and HACCP
- New Product Development
- Provide technical assistance in troubleshooting and investigations
- Coordinate new product requirements, trials schedules and technical support
- Generate Lactoferrin 101 sessions to bring awareness of the products to various departments
- Collaboration, facilitation of studies with research organizations

May 2013 – June 2015
RMIT University – School of Vocational Health & Sciences and School of Education
- Bridging Program Teacher at School of Vocation Health & Sciences – Cert III in Science & Cert IV in Tertiary Preparation in Science
- Planning, designing and delivering training for:
    - ICAICT105A Operate Spreadsheet Applications
    - ICAICT103A Use, communicate and search securely on the internet
    - Cert III in Science – VU21058 Use a range of techniques to solve mathematical problems
- Lecturing, tutoring and demonstrator for Health & Nutrition, Associate Degree in Health Science
- Demonstrator for Associate Degree in Applied Science
- Administrative assistance to create, edit, format training material for Project UNESCO
- Project SERRA – Creating a spreadsheet application for Students Electronic Records & Results
- Protein and Dairy Demonstrator for Dairy Science & Technology

Feb 2013 – Nov 2013
- SAP administrative roles – Citipower Powercor and Medibank Health Solution

June 2012 – Dec 2012
Fonterra Brands Australia – Process Technologist
- Working in conjunction with our corporate Product Development Team and leading the implementation of new product development onsite
- Successfully launched 2 products – 3.2kg Logs sold in Deli at Woolworths and 750g Woolworths Cheese slices
- Providing process improvement suggestions to site management team
- Updating operational product specifications
- Checking packaging material and all associated artwork prior to site approval
- Acting as the main contact with packaging and artwork suppliers regarding quality and printing issues
- Creating SAP Training Document during SAP implementation

Feb 2010 – June 2012
Murray Goulburn Co-operative Company Limited – Lactoferrin Process Coordinator and Product Technologist
- Working in conjunction with research scientist to implement new product and process in lactoferrin plant
- Co-ordinate commercial scale trials and provide feedback to the management
- Work with Quality department to update HACCP and implement corrective actions
- Gap analysis to identify the requirements for Therapeutic Goods Administration (TGA) license
- Updating and ensuring operators followed the required protocols for Standard Operating Procedures

Searching for Infinity

Jan 2008 – Mar 2009
Golden Circle – Food Scientist
- Investigating the use of a new packaging on the factory floor
- Assisting the R&D manager with patent work on pad absorption. Reviewing 1000+ patents
- Conducted an accelerated shelf-life testing for orange juice to determine the degradation of vitamin C
- Report on the browning of pineapple
- Sensory evaluation and detailed report to management on new product development – pineapple pieces and crush trialed in various juice combination
- Product reformulation for Popper Fizz

Nov 2005 – Jan 2008
Various office support and administrative roles – TRUenergy, Sparq Solutions, Bunnings HR, Alcan.

Oct 2003 – Oct 2005
Australian Starter Culture Research Centre – Cheese Science Applications Technologist
- A pioneering role in Australia to extend Australian Cheese Technology Projects to the cheese factories through commercializing pilot scale and implementing findings from research providers
- Responsibilities included familiarizing with the dairy industry, along with conducting factory trials – planning, executing and writing reports on the project completion.
- This role gave me a good experience to translate the research to the manufacturing environment via extension projects and also was a good opportunity to identify key issues or gaps affecting the Australian cheese industry

Dec 2001 – Sept 2003
Fonterra Co-operative Group Limited– Fonterra Graduate Technical Program (FGTP) &
Process Development Technologist (Cheese)
- As a graduate, I got an insight to the knowledge, applications and understanding of various dairy products, processes and technologies and presented on my factory visits and case studies.
- Research project on the development of high protein extruded snack using dairy proteins
- Masters' Research Project – Moisture variation in cheese
- Validate model, report writing and final presentation of my Masters project

Achievements & Awards

March – Nov 2018	Certificate in Small Business Management and Project Management
March 2018	Successful completion of Blanchard® Situational Leadership® II Training
July – Dec 2017	Certificate in Money Management, Te Wananga O Aoetearoa
	New Zealand Certificate in Personal Financial Capability and Financial Services (L3)
July 2013	Successful recipient of VET Scholarship Program. Higher Education and Skills Group funded Scholarship for Vocational Education Training (VET) teaching
July 2013	Cert IV in Training & Assessment. TAE 40110 RMIT University, Australia
2002 – 2003	Masters in Dairy Science & Technology (Hons) Massey University, New Zealand
May 2003	Fonterra Sponsorship for DIANZ Study Tour Queensland, Australia
1998 – 2001	Bachelor of Technology (Hons) in Food Technology Massey University, New Zealand

Memberships
Current — Dairy Industry Association of Australia (DIAA)

Interests
Hiking, writing, dancing, organizing and conducting cooking workshops

Referees
Upon request

Resume from Jaishree Ravindran for PhD at Charles Sturt University

For my cover letter, my career guidance counsellor – Graham Christensen (now a New Zealand artist) from Massey University – suggested the following format that I have often shared with many friends and family. I would like to take this opportunity to acknowledge and thank Graham Christensen for the career tips, techniques, and tools for writing a cover letter and presentation of the resume, also known as curriculum vitae.

Use the career brief to highlight where you want to be – your future aspirations. For example, the company you are applying for and why you want to work for that company.

The next paragraph should be your current situation, your expertise, experiences, and what can you bring to the role or the company.

The last and final paragraph should be about your past and more relevant experience and what makes you an ideal candidate – even for a role that may not be advertised.

Often, it's a good idea to have a complete long version of your career brief with all the juicy details and depending on the role you apply for, you can take the most relevant sections. It's like having your detailed career script and taking the relevant bits for the position applied.

There are several questions to prepare for an interview. This is how I do it:

1. Look at the company's vision, mission, products, values, and how they align with mine.
2. *Tell me about yourself.* Have this ready even when you are asked at 2am in the morning.

3. *Why should we take you?* This is 90% about you and 10% about the company and marry the two together.
4. *Why do you want to work for us?* This is 90% about the company and 10% about your skills that is transferable to the role. This is also an opportunity to showcase that you have studied about the company.
5. *When you are asked, do you have any questions for us?* Ask at least two questions – one about the role i.e. how is the career progression or what projects will I be working on as a Technologist? The second about the management or the company. This is your opportunity to interview to see if you really want to work for this manager and the company.
6. Knowing what is important to you and what you want in life is critical for your personal growth and excellence.
7. My strategy is to follow up **only** if you get feedback and learn what is required to be polished when applying for the next role.

While watching the Bollywood movie, *3 Idiots,* I liked the concept of 'follow excellence and success will follow you'. It is very true.

In the positions where I ran after a lucrative offer, the satisfaction was short-lived. In fact, I put myself under a lot of pressure. When I took on a role for the love of it, I remained happy and satisfied, yet we all seek that, *"Oh I wish I could earn a little more,"* conundrum in our head.

I will leave you with these questions:

What is important to you? How are you going to shape your life with what you have?

Splashes of Pink in My Life

What are you going to build with what you have?

My father often says, *"A contended mind is a continual feast."* To which I would like to add, an unsatisfied mind is a continual beast. The choice is yours for a feast or a beast!

When we are happy, we create a world of possibilities; whereas with frustration and agitation, the calmness of the mind is disturbed, and the clarity of mind becomes clouded. So keep clear at all times.

Time to seek your infinity...

1. What did you get out of this chapter?

　

2. What came to your heart, mind, and body as you read this chapter?

Splashes of Pink in My Life

3. What resonated with you?

_____

_____

_____

_____

_____

4. What would you like to share?

_____

_____

_____

_____

_____

5. What is your take home message?

_____

_____

_____

_____

_____

_____

Chapter Nine

Universal Truth

This chapter has been cooking in my head for a very long time and I often get very excited to share what I have discovered about *Universal Truth*. I will present this in various sections and pose questions along the chapter to take a deeper look into our lives.

Part One – Life is a Bed of Roses

My father has often said, *"Baby, life is not a bed of roses."*

Every time he said that, I would very diligently listen and acknowledge him and one day, the acceptance came in a form of a poem.

He saluted to my response and was blown away with my poem.

I replied, *"Daddy, life truly is a bed of roses."*

Life is nothing but bed of roses
For bed of roses are on top of the thorns
Is it for real or just a myth like beautiful white unicorns?

I need a strong sole and sturdy soul
To travel and unravel ... the journey of my life and my soul
There are multiple and various roles
Each teach me lessons to attain their goals

How do I innocently seal my fate?
How do I intelligently keep my heart open and gate?
Some experiences make me bitter
Until I realise it was to get me fitter
Some experiences make me happy
And some take me on a ride... topsy-turvy

Splashes of Pink in My Life

Some experiences are like the catalyst
Unbeknown at the time with eyes full of mist
Until I truly learn, acknowledge and transform
It haunts me until my mind goes back to norm

With these words, I unload the distress
For I like to travel light and carry less

Embracing my quirkiness
And living life with fullness

Only when we are content and happy, can we truly see the infinite possibilities within us. We need to rise above our problem to find its solution.

Daddy concluded, *"Contended mind is a continual feast."*

Feast indeed!

Part Two – Ruhi and Devotionals

Sahar often said she was doing Ruhi classes in the evening and I was curious. I thought they were short stories with morals. My favourite subject at school was Moral Science, where we had a story and at the end of each chapter, we had a moral of the story.

As a kid, I did not enjoy cartoons or comic books and rather preferred moral science while I patiently awaited the moral of the story. I have often thought of visiting my school in Bombay (now known as Mumbai) – Fatima High School in Vidhyavihar and getting the latest text books for reminiscing the knowledge and have a copy in my library.

Universal Truth

So, where were we? Ruhi!

The first book is called *Reflections on the Life of the Spirit* and has several units. The topics include understanding the Bahá'í writings, prayer, life and death.

The second book is called *Arising to Serve* and the contents include the joy of teaching, uplifting conversation, and deepening themes.

The purpose of the teachings is a two-fold path – intellectual and spiritual growth and for community service.

During our Ruhi sessions, Pooja, Sahar and I are able to have a deeper dive based on each unit and topic that we cover once a week.

We really get to know one another and connect on a spiritual level, too. I have longed and yearned to have friends with whom I can share some serious uplifting spiritual conversation and am grateful to Sahar and Pooja for the opportunity.

On a monthly basis, we also meet and catch up with other friends, XiangLan, Pravanjan, Henryk, Viv and any friends who were keen to catch up at our monthly meet ups. The occasion known as *Devotionals* – where the table at the restaurant is booked under Dev-O-Tease.

The purpose of our monthly Devotionals is to discuss a chosen topic. Sahar has the material for each topic. So far, the topics we have discussed are Unity, Trust, Purpose, Values, Ego, Freedom, and Detachment. The Devotionals have become a ritual that we look forward to each month.

For the chosen topic, we bring along any songs, quotes, or prayers. The Devotional begins with us sitting in a circle and starting with prayers. My prayer is *"Lokha Samastha Sukhino bhavantu, Lokha Samastha Sukhino bhavantu, Lokha Samastha Sukhino bhavantu. Om Shanti! Shanti! Shanti hee!"*

Loosely translating as, *"May there be happiness and peace in all beings!"*

Sahar says her prayer in Farsi, English or Arabic. I enjoy the phonetics and pronunciations of the prayers, though I speak neither Farsi nor Arabic.

During our monthly Devotionals, we discuss various quotes from a variety of spiritual leaders, famous philosophers, and including the founder of the Bahá'í faith (Bahá'u'lláh).

When we were discussing Values, I felt I got the golden key to unlock my inner potential. Many years ago, when I was looking for books on values, what are mine, how to cultivate, I felt lost and when I saw this, it was an ah-ha, eureka moment!

I am very happy to share with you the very simple, yet powerful learning I received, and with persistence, we can open up a world of infinite possibilities – including universal truth!

"Your beliefs become your thoughts,
Your thoughts become your words,
Your words become your actions,
Your actions become your habits,
Your habits become your values,
Your values become your destiny."
(Mahatma Gandhi)

I really enjoy the above quote as it lays the foundation and pathway, step-by-step to both your values and your destiny.

As friends, we get a glimpse into our thoughts that we share openly and value our diversity – we are very accepting of each other. We also ask how we are going to implement these into our personal lives.

We all come from different countries, backgrounds, religions and have an open discussion on our thoughts on the various topics and see the unity through our diversity – especially how we are going to implement the topic of discussion into our day-to-day personal or professional lives.

When discussing a new topic each month, we openly share our thoughts and views and really get to know the people on a spiritual level, get an insight into the inner worlds – while realising that although we come from different faiths, how harmoniously we create a mutual understanding.

We can, at times, debate and have disagreed with one another, yet we conclude in harmony and understand that there is more than one way to look at something. As a result mutual respect and adoration have built over time.

Part Three – Your Family Matters

As far as the cartoons are concerned, as an adult, I am fascinated by their technicalities, the animation, and the imagination of the creator. The only cartoons I thoroughly enjoyed as a kid were superheroes. Spiderman, for its catchy song and He-Man and how with the power of his sword Cringer was transformed to a mighty BattleCat – a fearless tiger.

Splashes of Pink in My Life

On Sunday mornings, I would often sing the title song with my brother as the programme started on the television. By now, you can tell how I tend to go into a rabbit hole of memories and I reminisce the journey thoroughly.

Yes, I've always been a huge Bruce Lee fan as I used to watch his movies when I visited my grandparents in my native place in Chitlapakkam, India.

I had an amazing childhood and have beautiful memories with my brother, Anand. I have adored him and looked up to him and we have had friendly competitions – including how many countries we've visited. We have inspired one another through our lives and I'm very grateful to have him as my brother in my life.

When my brother got married, I dedicated this poem to my sister-in-law, affectionately known as *Vodhiney* (in Telugu) or *Bhabhi* (in Hindi).

Sad to be leaving
(but) glad to be going
So is life
When you become a wife
With lots of memories to take
And future ones to make
So is life
When you become a wife
Mixed emotions
In little portions
Come and go
Sometimes high
Sometimes low
So is life

When you become a wife
Think no further
Oh wife of my dear brother
Just enjoy the ride
Leaving the thoughts aside
But do remember, so is life
When you become a wife
Making a nest of your own
New seeds to be sown
Beginning a new life
In a form of a beautiful wife
So is life
When you become a wife

The moral from this part is that your family really cares for you, your well-being, and are your well-wishers. No matter the distance. Being mindful of our needs and the respect we have; we can only blossom in love.

I would also like to take this opportunity to acknowledge my grandfather whom I admire and revered. My grandfather was a very progressive man. Lovingly, all the grandchildren referred to him as Thatha or DK Thatha.

Thatha was a vivid reader, a very highly disciplined man, either walking, cycling, reading, gardening, simply enjoying his chai tea or catching up with family.

Every summer, Thatha would visit us. And summer meant, I got to revise Maths and English with Thatha. He taught me the Vedic technique of finding the square of any number ending in five. I loved learning this knowledge from him and still use the Vedic method today.

Thatha was a wireless operator in the Indian Railways and this was in the 1930s. His mother, Kannamma, was a dynamic lady and my mother's mother, Sampath, was a very charming lady.

My father raves so much about my mother's mother; I'm in awe and also in sadness that she departed before my arrival on planet earth.

Thatha believed deeply in education, so much so he would travel to great lengths to ensure all his children got the best education from the best institute.

This is an extract from my grandfather's journal about my great grandfather who had served in World War I.

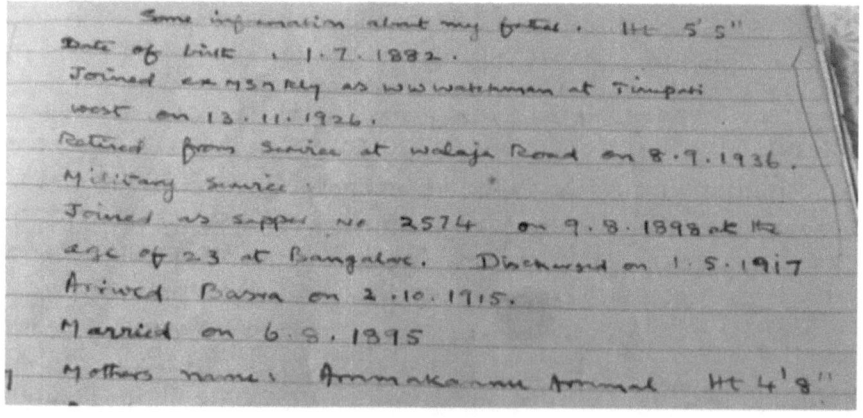

Excerpt from DK Thatha's journal

My mother is an embodiment of discipline and she has imparted this in me throughout life – be it the kitchen or living a simple, peaceful life.

I have learnt many things from my parents and often, my mother will say, *"What we know is only a handful and what we do not know is ocean full."*

There is a saying in Tamil for that:

"Therinjadhu kai alavu, theriyadhadhu kadal alavu."

In English, this means that the unknown not only brings humility but also curiosity to know and learn more.

Today, whenever I have a challenge or problem, I would recall what my father says about defining the problem. By defining the problem, I feel we rise above the problem and emotionally detach from the problem. Then, put the tools into play to mitigate the problem.

My father often says, *"Remember one thing in life. Yes, there are many 'one things' in life, so do not make a commitment when you are happy and do not a make a decision when you are emotional."*

The response to a question my mother had asked me when I was in Sydney back in 2000, *"Is there anything that you would like me to change about myself?"*

All I had was this poem as a response, nine years later on her birthday in 2009.

Splashes of Pink in My Life

My dear dearest divine mother ...
You are a beautiful wife of my lovely father
Wonderful and delightful mother of my beloved brother
You are source of inspiration
Life in life of respiration
And unsolved mystery
Just perfect chemistry
You have endowed dispassion
Yet with love in superb fashion
Your beauty is a maze
Am stuck and still in gaze
You are the awareness of the breath
Deep devotion, divinity in the ultimate depth
Where you are, there is fun
Words, deep meanings with lots of pun
Am blessed to be your beloved daughter
May the divine encompass you in joy and laughter
When I wake up in the morning
Motherly hug is your Baby longing
When I go to sleep at night
I know my mother is just right
You cannot be replaced
Without you I am misplaced
I wonder why God made me your daughter
Because no words can explain this matter!

And here is a poem I wrote for my father, lovingly I call him Daiddee, my achaa Daddy:

You personify dedication to work
You personify persistence and hard-work
You personify doing your research and homework
By defining the problem – what is the problem

You mitigate and eliminate them
And thus, easily problems are overcome
For me (and Anand) ... you are our perfect Daiddee
Always spick, span, clean and so tidy!

We love you so much
Words are not enough to express as such
My acchha Daiddee
You are the bestest Daiddee

Part Four – Lessons from Geometry

When I was in ninth standard, we learnt about theorems in geometry.

The infinite lines through a point depicts infinite ways to do things, infinite thoughts, and opinions of people. Yet the 'one' point is the perceiver.

These are some of my favourites that also form part of the Universal Truth. You can draw infinite lines through a point – I depict this like the rays of sun.

However, how many straight lines can you draw through two points?

The answer is one.

Yes, if you're being a smarty pants, you could say infinite squiggly lines – hence the question, how may straight lines through two points?

The journey between the start and end of line is one – the voyage of my life.

I also enjoyed the fact that the sum of all angles in a triangle is 180 degrees and a straight line also has 180 degrees.

Another theorem that I enjoyed is that every square is a rectangle but not every rectangle is a square.

Part Five - Universal Truth and Innovation

Every summer holidays, my parents bought books of our choice. I was not a veracious reader and I thought cartoons were childish, so I didn't enjoy them then.

I was interested in serious topics, such as philosophy, from a very young age. The library was accessible only at school and not during school holidays. During school holidays we would gather in the evening and play outdoor games.

At school we had a choice of books – the boys would choose *Hardy Boys* and the girls would choose *Nancy Drew*. There were other books like the *Famous Five*.

None of them fascinated me as much as *Akbar and Birbal*; witty, funny, with questions and brilliant outside-the-box answers.

Later in life, I discovered *Akbar and Birbal for Management Problems*. I enjoy them and reminisce the stories no matter how many times I've read them! I love the way Akbar would ask questions and Birbal did his research for the answers.

As a child, my brother and I had a collection of books from many summers, I wanted to bring this opportunity to other kids. We lived in Damodhar Park in Ghatkopar. There were many buildings. Each building had 11 or 12 floors and each floor had four houses.

So, when I was 12, I took the initiative and created a brochure and placed it in the elevator area of the buildings.

Each morning, I lit a lamp that I had created in another Personal Development Programme and started my own mini library.

Depending on the type of book, I either lent it for 50 paise or some novels for 1 rupee. This was back in the early 90s.

To my surprise, I earned 200 rupees in the summer of 1991, which was a large sum of money for a twelve-year-old.

I often tap into this experience when I am nervous about being an entrepreneur or doing something innovative or out of the box.

The lesson I learnt and reflect on often is to go out there and have fun! With the 200 rupees, I bought two tops, a tailor-made yellow frilled dress. I had one of the tops for over 25 years.

The Games we Played

When we lived in Bombay, each evening, a bunch of girls would gather and play games. In summer, the sun would set around 7pm and after that, we would sit and sing songs or play seated games.

In the evening when the sun was still up, we would play other games like hide and seek, kings, and many more. I have included some of the games that I recollect and reminisce in the back of this book.

I added this as part of the collection of childhood memories and potential lessons that we can learn as adults and have fun in the process. See section *The Games We Played As Kids*.

Part Six – Places of Worship

I would like to acknowledge *Gurudwaras* around the world. The ones I have visited are the ones in Christchurch, Melbourne, and Shepparton. I have found peace and solace in every visit to a Gurudwara.

I often loved introducing people to the Gurudwara. There was a point in my life where I was hungry, and all I wanted was food and solace and I found this in Gurudwara.

I would rock up after work to the Gurudwara and sit there, pray, meditate, shed tears, and then in the kitchen, be fed hot and freshly cooked meals by the volunteers.

No questions, no talking, it felt like a silent conversation between the Guru (Master) and me.

As a gesture of thank you, I wanted to serve and return my gratitude and I got this opportunity in other places. I introduced Salsa Cris to Gurudwara and we both enjoyed the food and often had great in-depth, meaningful conversations.

I do not remember the details of the conversations, but I do remember the feeling of elation. I often took flowers, rice, or milk and donated it to the Gurudwara. Rice is an auspicious material offered in marriages for good wishes, milk is for longevity and flowers were my way of expressing my tender feelings and offering them to God.

Part Seven – American Field Services (AFS), Austausch Schulerin in der Schweiz

When I was eight years old, my brother went to boarding school and I wanted to experience that, too. Call me weird but I really wanted to! I wanted to go to another place, live the culture, and experience life in a new light. I had this opportunity through American Field Services (AFS).

After a rigorous interview process, I was selected to go on an international cultural exchange program. It had been only a few months since we had immigrated to New Zealand and I filled in an application form from the junk mail.

My parents supported me and friends helped to take me to the location where the interview was happening.

In July 1995, when my father was in India, and I was with my mother and brother in New Zealand, I got the news that I had passed the interview process.

I was awarded the opportunity to represent New Zealand as an international exchange student.

I wanted to go to Switzerland not for the cheese or chocolate but for *Maggi*. *Maggi*, a brand owned by *Nestle*, and the headquarters of *Nestle* was Switzerland, so I wanted to go to the land of *Maggi* noodles! Ironically, I didn't find any *Maggi* noodles or instant noodles when I was in Switzerland.

I had my wish come true and have often sought inspiration from this time when I start a new task and have no clarity or the logical steps ahead.

I had no savings or a job or any monetary funds, yet I was determined to go. I knew I was going and did not know how.

I applied to many companies, wrote several letters but nothing to avail. As a child, my spirit did not break because I got a rejection, I kept working diligently and the scholarships came through in other ways. When I look at this story, I realise that we give our best shot where we can, and the answer or solution surely comes but not necessarily through the same source from where we are seeking.

I got three scholarships, one from AFS itself, the other from Oliver Stoddard Scholarship, and a third from my school Mt Roskill Grammar School, Auckland. I got a part-time job as a packer in a local supermarket, Food Town (now Countdown), and my first manager was a tall Swedish lady, Inga.

I am grateful for Inga who gave me as many shifts as possible and slowly I saw the dollars started adding up. My mother also made snacks like *murukku* and I sold them outside the library. My father helped me with fund raising events and we sold *batada wada* (deep fried spiced potato in a batter) outside the supermarkets.

I am forever grateful to my host family (Familie Bernhard) in Switzerland. I still call my host parents *Mom* and *Dad*. My host Dad passed away in 2020 and due to the COVID-19 pandemic, I was unable to visit. My host Dad was a walking encyclopedia of the history and culture of Switzerland.

I was able to express my deepest gratitude when I heard he had a short time to live and was in the hospital. I have been in awe of my host parents and have imparted several 'travel' habits from them that I hold very dear in my heart and implement whenever I travel.

When my host family came to know the student that they were going to host is originally from India and the religion that I followed was Hinduism, my host parents borrowed books from the library about Hinduism to gain a deeper understanding to make me feel comfortable.

When I departed from New Zealand on my exchange year, I looked up to my host parents as my parents, so I called them Mom and Dad. My host Mom would often introduce me to many people that I was their *'Dochter'* (daughter) for the year and 20 years later, now I am referred as their *'Indische Dochter'* (Indian daughter).

I came to know about my host Dad's last moments only a few hours before he departed his body. Although he did not speak, I expressed my love and gratitude towards him. I have tears as I write this.

My host parents and siblings have had a huge impact on my life and I'm forever grateful for the experiences that live evergreen in my memory. If you ask me to get ready in minutes, the credit goes to my host mom. She has a book filled with the various countries they have travelled to. Through my host family, I got to experience and live a crazy and quirky life!

Even after so many years, whenever I visit Wetzikon, the town I lived in, I find it astonishing that the train timetables have not changed much and there is still the S5 express train to Zurich HauptBanhof. I remember getting frustrated when the transport system in other places were not as efficient as the SwissBahn!

My host parents have visited me once in New Zealand, in India and also in Melbourne, Australia. The experiences and cultural exchange have been priceless. Our families are connected too.

You might be wondering, why is this in the Universal Truth?

As I grapple and put this into words, I realise that there is an understanding at a family level – even if the families are apart, this brings peace and harmony. This was the purpose of the AFS Exchange Program – to develop global citizens! And I can see how this is in play. I got to know, live, and experience another culture and was even more fortunate to have been looked after by Familie Bernhard.

My host parents and host siblings gave me rich experiences of Switzerland and we deeply value the relationship that we have built over two decades.

AFS Exchange Year with Familie Bernhard

Universal Truth

Part Eight – Community Service at Tatura Community House

When the COVID-19 pandemic hit, I wanted to help the community and offered to make meals and deliver to the nominated households. When Goulburn Valley was hit hard with the pandemic and almost 50% of the population were in isolation, I had the opportunity to serve my community.

I made about 30 meals based on what was available in the Community House. I like to be surprised with the ingredients and come up with a unique meal, like the *Iron Chef*.

When I was in New Zealand and had started writing, I left my position with the intention to travel around the world and write this book. So, when I visited one of the colleagues and his partner for dinner – Simon and Su, we cooked a meal together, shared stories and I shared that this is what I was going to do.

Stay at a friend's house, be surprised with the ingredients and make a meal together, like the *Ready Steady Cook* on TV. And so, for the dinner at Su and Simon's place, we came up with the creative innovation of pasta and egg curry that we all thoroughly enjoyed.

After spending time with Simon and Su, I requested them to write in my scrapbook. I carry a scrapbook where I request people to write in it. During times of joy, or even sadness, when I look at the book, it lifts me up, lifts my spirit, and I reminisce the good old times with people who have written in my book. I asked Simon and Su to give me a chapter to write about. I was given a chapter title that I loved so much that I made it the title of this book: *Splashes of Pink in my Life*.

Thank you, Simon and Su.

Now let's fast forward many years, and on track to Tatura Community House and serving during the pandemic.

After making about 30 odd meals, I delivered the meals to the homes of people who were impacted by the pandemic and the people were either nominated or put their hand up for food packages.

After delivering the meals, I got many text messages wishing and blessing me and my family for the service. I felt very humbled and continued on without thinking much. It was an experience where I felt good and yet humble! It was a feeling of thank you for giving me the opportunity to help and serve to the community I was living in.

Fast forward many months, when I learnt the community manager was moving on and it was her last day, I personally went to wish my heartfelt thanks for giving me the opportunity for the cooking workshop which was a huge success and also the opportunity to be a helping hand to volunteer during the pandemic.

That is when I learnt that the Tatura Community was nominated for the Goulburn Valley Volunteer Award. I felt such joy. I would like to acknowledge and thank my parents, the company I worked for (Bega Cheese in Tatura) due to which I lived in the Goulburn Valley community, and to the Tatura Community House for the opportunity to serve.

Universal Truth

Serving in the Tatura Community House during the pandemic

Part Nine – Dhamma Server at Vipassana

Having done Vipassana, I wanted to serve. I was overjoyed with gratitude with the accommodation and amazing food that we all received the first time I did Vipassana in Auckland, New Zealand.

I made it an utmost requirement that I serve the Vipassana community. The first time I had this opportunity was in

December 2020. I volunteered for the work period where we got the place ready for the upcoming 10-day silent retreat.

Activities included cleaning and getting the hall ready, cooking, gardening and any help as required. I went prepared thinking it will be another silent retreat – no speaking, etc.

However, we were allowed to talk, and it was a pleasant experience. I wanted to volunteer again in August 2021 for a 10-Day course (silent retreat), however due to the lockdown and Woori Yallock being in metro, Melbourne was under lockdown, too. The retreat was cancelled, I shortened my holiday and life went on.

In 2022, I had the opportunity to volunteer and I did so for three days – arriving on Monday evening after Easter holidays and departing on Thursday morning. When my roommate with whom I shared the room went offline – I gave that a go, too.

I was too excited the night I arrived and did not sleep. Yes, that's how quirky I am. When our energy levels are so high, we are ecstatically happy, and we bounce like little children. That's exactly how I felt. I want to be of service to the Vipassana community.

I was happy to clean the toilets and create an atmosphere of hygiene with so much gratitude! It is amazing how the Vipassana Centre works. The kitchen has a manager, and the female and male sides each have managers. And I enjoyed serving the servers. I got an insight into the way of Vipassana, how the meals are all done on time, the planning involved, how to ensure there is minimal or no waste; a perfect blend of noble speech and noble silence.

Universal Truth

It is easier to be silent than be in a blend of noble speech and silence. Here I was thinking that I am contributing to the community, but the reality as I saw, was overwhelming joy and gratitude that I had tears for the opportunity and really felt how the Universe had my back and was looking after me!

As I departed the Vipassana Centre and bowed down and kissed the earth, I was extremely grateful for the joy, bliss, and gratitude I felt.

Part Ten - Landmark Worldwide

This book has been made possible due to many unique people, situations and circumstances. And a key one has been Landmark. I have included this in the Universal Truth chapter for several reasons. This book has been part of my Self Expression Leadership Program (SELP) community project.

I signed up for Landmark (https://www.landmarkworldwide.com/) with two clear intentions: to write my book and start my PhD.

I had heard about Landmark through *138 Dates* by Rebekah Campbell. Rebekah had done the Landmark Forum and I was so moved, touched, and inspired that I wanted to do this as part of my personal development.

I got in touch with Rebekah after I had finished listening to her audiobook. Rebekah connected with me and responded to my questions, too.

Similar to Vipassana, I did not do any research about Landmark, I rang the centre and said I wanted to sign up. I signed up the following day on 11th November to keep it memorable. The way Landmark works is through ontology. Through sharing, the Forum Leader guides us to take a look into our own lives and through a step-by-step process, I discovered immense, profound experiences.

I have found it difficult to share and often say that it is like you have this amazing dish in front of you and there is no point describing it to great lengths when you need to experience it for yourself.

I really understood who I was, what were the stories running in my head, what was the impact and patterns in life where I was playing small, how was I compensating in my life. And from a place of awareness, I had the possibility to be free. When you choose you choose!

I had several breakthroughs in life and the next level has been that of community. What am I striving for? What is my project for the community and how is this helping the community?

This has been a community project for me and I am writing it because:

- I have embraced a community project as part of my self-expression as a community leader.
- The pandemic has affected several people in all walks of their life, especially our mental health. If no action is taken, we will continue to be isolated! The way the future could be in this area if a new possibility was created was to share our lives, lessons we have learnt within ourselves and our communities. This is an extended community work that the book will empower young

Universal Truth

adults, global citizens, and any reader to be courageous, connected, celebrate, embrace awareness and the global community we live in for the significance of connection and humanity.
- I want this to be a go-to book for anyone, including myself seeking inspiration, recipes, and glimpses of my life.
- It has been a lifelong dream and keeping my word to be an international published author.

I got a lot out of Landmark's program – how to embrace and take a sneak peek into the don't know of the don't knows. It is a blind spot that requires reflection, what it really means to be a leader – to make an impact, connect and truly connect with people on a deeper level.

What I got out of community project is practising the connection, what it means to be in a community, how am I the representative of my community, what are the possibilities, and who am I being out there in the world?

One of the many things that I learnt from Landmark was having a mentor and I know they have my back. I had the feeling of *"Yadhumm Oorey, yavarum kayleer."*

My mother has told me about the sentence, *"Yadhumm Ooray Yaavarum Kayleer"* and I could see it unfold in Landmark. The meaning that *"I belong to everyone and all places"* – I am a global citizen and the members are my family.

In his speech at the European Union in 2015, Dr Abdul Kalam has spoken about this and what it means for humanity. For me, it meant, I belong to the world, and all the people are my family.

This is what it takes to be a global citizen.

After listening to Brené Brown's *Braving the Wilderness*, I actually came to understand what it meant when Maya Angelou said, *"You only are free when you realize you belong no place — you belong every place — no place at all. The price is high. The reward is great."*

Dr APJ Kalam continued in his speech, *"As we say in India, where there is righteousness in the heart, there is beauty in the character. When there is beauty in the character, there is harmony in the home. Where there is harmony in the home, there is an order in the nation. When there is order in the nation, there is peace in the world."*

So, here is an opportunity, dear reader. If ever you feel small, if ever you feel insignificant, go help another person, help the community, and you will feel like a drop in the ocean and at the same time, feel the immensity of being the ocean yourself!

Here are some of the places for opportunity to volunteer or feel purposeful:

1. Your local community – a chance to shine what sings to your heart and shine your light. In a recent podcast by Jay Shetty, *On Purpose*, he interviewed Mirranda Kerr. An incredible and an amazing woman. As I listened to her, I realised how judgemental I had been and was able to transform and see through her beauty and intelligence. Jay Shetty has shared many of his knowledge, wisdom, and tools in his book, *Think Like a Monk* – what an amazing life! I like the parts he talks about trust and the different levels of trust, and what it means to be compatible in a relationship.

2. Your local place of worship. I have often visited SAI SIVA VISHNU Temple and volunteered when the temple was being formed. Whenever I had spiritual questions, the temple founder Guru Rajaramji (Guruji) has clarified my doubts, questions, and helped me understand the spiritual traditions and clarified the consciousness. More information is available on https://srisaisivavishnutemple.com/

3. Talking to our neighbours. We get to know about the community we live in.

When we are ready to offer our help, the university opens infinite possibilities for our growth and development. This chapter is the reason for the book.

When you read and practise your own self-development programme, it all boils down to service.

I often ask myself, what have I learnt and how can I implement them in my life? Be it personal, professional or everyday walk of life.

How can I walk the talk that I listened to? I like being a role model and have often strived too hard. When I realise I need to drop it, and be at peace within myself, I feel life is effortless and simply smooth sailing.

Chapter Nine has many questions along the way, so here are some more questions for you...

1. What talents are you willing to extend to contribute to your community?

_____

_____

_____

_____

_____

2. How often would you like to volunteer?

_____

_____

_____

_____

3. What would you like to share from your service experiences?

_____

_____

_____

_____

_____

_____

4. What would enhance you to contribute to your community?

_____

_____

_____

_____

_____

Chapter Ten

The Journey to PhD

I have wanted to do a PhD for many reasons, and it has taken me almost 20-odd years to get out of my own way!

I have had several attempts of doing a PhD, but why a PhD? Why the degree in Doctor of Philosophy? I get goose bumps far more about the 'Philosophy' part more than the 'Doctor' part.

Was I here to achieve a name for myself, to prove my intelligence? Why the PhD? It has taken me almost nine years to find the topic or perhaps the topic to find me… and acknowledge the whole concept or *funda* (said in a strong Indian accent) about my PhD.

Yes, I acknowledge and like the Dr in front of my name to become Dr. Jaishree Ravindran, not to be confused with a medical doctor, though I have suggested herbal remedies to medical doctors.

After having done Ayurvedic Cooking through the Art of Living, I learnt a lot. I started experimenting and observing myself and my surroundings and seeing the impact of food on mind and body.

There was a moment in my life, when I was asked, where do you want to be in five years?

The answer popped up in my head but I was too afraid to share it. I knew and wanted to do a PhD and was afraid to vocalise it. I was afraid of the impact that it may have on my current life.

More than anything, it was a way of being. When we finish something, it is not sad, it is a start of something new, something so profound.

I once bought a T-shirt for my father that read "CONFIDENCE – *the feeling you have before you fully understand the situation.*"

I had a glimpse of that in 2018 and I was few days from starting my PhD. It felt like my head and heart was going in opposite directions. So, I continued working in the industry. I do not know how things will unfold as things are moving at a rapid pace. By the time you are reading this book, I hope, pray, and intend to be doing the PhD.

You could say that this chapter is a cliff hanger!

Before I proceed, I would like to ask **YOU**, have you had a moment or moments in life where the head and the heart were in opposite directions?

What or how did you tackle the situation?

Most humans go with the head – it is logical and is usually the most obvious thing. The ones who want rapid transformation, want to leap into the unknown go for their heart. And I admit to having done both. At times where I have had a deep dive, where there were no expectations, I got a lot more than the situations where I've tiptoed.

I found my next piece of the puzzle when I got the news I have received the scholarship for my PhD.

Lactoferrin is an iron bound protein found in milk and it is my utmost passion to bring awareness of this sparkly pink, high-value protein to as many people as I come across in my life.

I now acknowledge being an expert while at the same time, I know there is still so much to learn, apply, discover, and transform.

The Journey to PhD

My justification for being one of the lactoferrin experts is that I have a strong network of lactoferrin experts. There are about 30 lactoferrin factories around the world, and I have worked for three companies while being involved in four factories.

I have been working in this field of lactoferrin for over nine years and the product has been commercially available only for 30 odd years. Yes, specialist would be more suitable I feel.

Out of my own initiative, I created the Rav-o-Meter and AmR-o-Meter. Yes, there are personal reasons for the name choices, too. Rav-o-Meter after my father's name (Ravindran) and AmR-o-Meter after my mother's name, Amudha.

The Rav-o-Meter and AmR-o-Meter can predict the level of lactoferrin in the milk and it is simple and easy to work with.

The fight between the head and the heart reminds me of a poem that I had written for my brother and my Bhabhi (sister-in-law) for their first wedding anniversary:

Dil se ... Jaan se
Woh jo dimaag samjhe
Shayad dil ko sambhale
Woh jo dil ko samjhe
Woh dimaag ko kya samjhaye
Issi sambhal samjhne mein
zindagi sajaayee jaati hai
Jab dimaag ko pata lagta hai
Jab dimaag ko mehsoos hota hai
Pal-pal suhana lagta hai!

Moving forward and reflecting, why do I want to a PhD?

I had five reasons.

When I finished my role as a Lactoferrin Development Technologist, I achieved five things: GRAS status, Liquid Lactoferrin, the Rav-o-Meter, the Lactoferrin Project that encompassed – manufacturing, sales, and technical – and a fifth one that was work in progress.

Lactoferrin is allowed to be added to infant formula in China and other countries, but why not in Australia and New Zealand?

The paperwork and effort seem too much, and I have often wondered why don't the companies come together and propose this to Food Standards Australia New Zealand (FSANZ).

Similarly, the reason why I wanted to do a PhD:

1. Benefit the university (in Australasia – I want to connect Australia and New Zealand) through my research.
2. Benefit the global lactoferrin industry and address a fundamental question – my research topic.
3. Benefit the Australasian economy – most of the lactoferrin manufacturers are in Australia and New Zealand – *Bega, Synlait, Saputo, Noumi, Beston, Provico, Fonterra, Tatua, Westland (Yili), Oceania (Yili)*.
4. Benefit the companies, including the community I live in – how it will manifest will be unfolded as a life-long journey. There are many possibilities to add value, create opportunities, inspire and empower the people in my life.
5. For myself – my aim and ambition to complete the highest qualification as a Doctorate and have a Dr in front of my name and become a lecturer in university, impart my knowledge, wisdom and share my experiences with fellow colleagues, researchers, and students.

The Journey to PhD

I read *The Secret of the Red Crystals* by Dr Sujatha Sharma that put me on track and empowered me to take the journey of PhD. I connected with Dr Sujatha Sharma via *LinkedIn* and that has opened up a realm of possibilities, too.

Here are some of the questions and hurdles I faced. I invite you to look into your own life, where you feel you have been stopped, or got stuck into a story in your head.

1. Who will pay your mortgage?
2. How are you going to live your life from having a good income to a student income?
3. You are in your 40s, what will happen after you finish your PhD, and who will give you a job?
4. Who are you depending on – financially, and emotionally?
5. Why do you want to do a PhD?
6. Are you being a responsible adult?
7. Why don't you do your PhD after you have paid off your mortgage?
8. Why do you want to study in that university?
9. And the list goes on.

Having worked for three out of many lactoferrin manufacturers, there is a recurring theme here! Finding a solution and adding value to the waste stream would help the lactoferrin manufacturers – not only in Australia and New Zealand but all the manufacturers of this valuable pink protein!

What I really got out of this whole experience is that when we get out of our own way, life is joyful, fun and unstoppable like a flowing gushing river. We stand on the river bank, yet the river is ever changing and evolving from moment to moment!

Splashes of Pink in My Life

Sometimes, there is a lot of dust to see our reflection in the mirror, and in the process of transformation, it can feel painful. I say it is worth it; just like reaching the top of a summit and seeing the vastness from top of a hill.

What I have learnt in life is the holy trinity of resources (people, money), time and energy. The concept of following time, money, or energy, I first heard it from a friend Daniel Batten.

When I follow time, I feel I do not have enough time, and when I follow money or focus on money, I find I do not have enough money.

However, when I follow what gives me energy, I find both resources, and time are put in place and things go in a flow.

Now, time to reflect on your own journey...

1. What did you get out of this chapter?

   _____

   _____

   _____

   _____

   _____

2. What came to your heart, mind, and body as you read this chapter?

   _____

   _____

   _____

   _____

   _____

Splashes of Pink in My Life

3. What resonated with you most in this chapter?

_____

_____

_____

_____

_____

4. What would you like to share from this chapter?

_____

_____

_____

_____

_____

5. What is your take home message from this chapter?

_____

_____

_____

_____

_____

_____

Chapter Eleven

Collection of Poems

These are my poems that I have written over many years and I believe this is a perfect opportunity to share and reveal them to the world.

Some lost, some kept and some untold.

Each poem has a story behind its inspiration and these memories are a momentum of discoveries and learnings.

Please enjoy.

Splashes of Pink in My Life

To Lovers for a New Beginning
18 June 2022

You are my diamond and I am your gold
And I feel like a diamond with your jewels I hold
Each day a new beginning as the magical stories unfold

Your tender kisses, touches are supple and soft
Like grazing grace in the universal loft
Your eyes are deeper than the depths of the sea
Your smile and presence embedded deep within me
Your warm hands keep me sheltered
Like the prayer in my heart that have melted
I feel closer to you than ever before
Free and captured in your arms even more

I am looking forward to spending the rest of our lives
To co-create infinite love and bind in worldly family ties
I secretively pray with hope and faith
Awaiting answer for the proposal to saith
For your answer to the proposal I have raiseth

You bring out the best in me through your devotion
I see the best in you and want that as a life-long dedication

Will I Ever Know?
3 April 2016

Will I ever know
How and when will I love myself?

Will I ever know
How and when will I realise my potentials?

Will I even know
When will my last day be on planet Earth?

Will I ever know
What secrets and legacy will I leave behind?

Will I ever know
What and how people felt about me?

Will I ever know
What am I truly meant to be?

Will I ever know
When, how, where, who is/was my soulmate meant to be?

Have I already found, lost and found myself again?

Will I ever know... I wonder if I will ever know
For the answers, I wait in vain
I simply say to myself... "You never know, Jai! You may never know."

Splashes of Pink in My Life

A Response to a Poem
14 February 2016

In response to the poem 'Beyond All Relationships'

When I'll be dead...
Don't let sad tears shed,
let the joyful ones flow instead
Coz by now you would know...
How curious I was to know about life, after am dead

You will send flowers...
Show love n its powers
To someone alive instead!

Don't appreciate n praise me when I am alive
Save them when I am dead
Else those words will boast my ego n get a big head
Praise me later, instead!

Constructively criticise my faults
They are my boost n malt
Tell them now while am still alive,
To help me improve now in life
No use when you tell them when I am dead
Tell them now, instead!

Get a life, keep yourself busy, don't let your mind wander n miss me
Coz life goes on, kiss me on my forehead
While am still alive n not when am dead

You'll want to say Love You...
Don't say it too quickly

Let the heart grow fonder
N mysteries will grow n ponder
N life will blossom n wonder!
Save it for later instead.

You'll wish...
You could have spent more time with me...
Let that feeling be!
It will only make me very special in your heart
Let that feeling grow, instead!

"Spend time with every person around you, your families, friends, more so with you, coz that is the only person you will see after life in another life!

Life is good, just strive for the best
Be the better version of yourself
Remember good is the enemy of the best.
Love yourself before you love anybody else!

Evolution of the Emotional Mind
26 October 2016

I have been longing and yearning
for an unknown deeply within me burning

When emotions went hay-wire
Like an uncontrolled blazing fire

When expectations not fulfilled
frustration turned into anger
Digging deep I discovered
emotions unmodulated were a danger
clouding judgements and even logic
ego, pride, attitudes that were very toxic

Confusion, conflict ... nothing but contradictions
Counterintuitive were supposed to be my actions
Approach and express rather than awaiting actions

Reach if you want to be reached
Approach if you want to be approached
Open myself if I want people to be open

Jotted all the words and feelings with a pen
As a placard of my emotional evolution
A firm resolution I wanted for my turmoil and isolation
modulating my expressions, needs and expectations.

Laws of Attraction
September 2013

For a guy it is very suffocating
When he is not reciprocating
To the love, when the girl is the one expressing
Her feelings even prior to his own feelings

This sort of attraction is only short-lived
Ever lasting mutual is the one to be prized
This is from the laws of attraction, one in the nature
This is how we procreate as a human creature

When the physics is unified with the chemistry
After a prolonged time it becomes history
Anything in a hurry, ends up being a short story!
This is life. Love – it ain't no mystery!

Developing a good friendship
Is the best way to start any relationship
If there is anything more than this
Let it simmer, don't give it a miss

As time passes by, let the mind take a disguise
Let the love, blossom and flourish in the eyes
Let him express his feelings for you
Then take your time to express yours too
This is the best way to courtship and romance
This is the best way a man likes to dance!

Splashes of Pink in My Life

Soul, My Sole Companion
September 2013

First run after name, place, power and things
Second over family, friends in circle and rings

Running stopped for all of the above
When I blossomed in my own love

Each relishing, walking their own path
Left to figure out what was my math

Once blossomed it is impossible to return
To the state of innocence in which we are born

I draw myself, yet fail to capture
Because the drawing exceeds my nature

Astonished! Am I really that beautiful?
Or is it the view of glass half full

Bewildered by the beauty of life
I am the soul (sole) - companion of my life!

If My Words
September 2013

Often I have thought if my words hurt you
Do I ignore, walk away or just not speak?
I now rethink ... if my words hurt you
I see this as a chance for me to tweak
If my words hurt you
It is a chance to speak out unresolved conflict
I surely have no intentions to cause hurt or pain to inflict
If my words hurt you
I see it as a chance to grow
Expressing or picking up feelings am no pro
Overtime the experience will prove or show
When my words do hurt you
I have a request for you to do
Ask – has she had the exposure?
Ask – is the question from a heart pure?
May be you do or may be you don't
Know why I am so self-critical of me
In the process have I only burnt
It has only harmed and set pain in me
I have no expectation from you
Your moral support is what takes me through
All I ask is speak your heart direct to me too
I know being over-protected
Makes me take things for granted
Only at times like these of pain
I realise how lucky, oh what a brain!
Through the poem I express my feelings
As a self-reminder, a lesson of my life's dealings

Splashes of Pink in My Life

I am Sorry
September 2013

*I have no intention of hurting you
With thoughts, words or even actions to mention a few*

*I do my best to refine every time
To overcome my fear and making it sublime
May be trying too hard makes it like a sour lime!*

*Every time, I fear I may hurt you
and withdraw myself away from you*

*When I realise the fear is dominating
more than life lessons that are awaiting
I slowly come out of my cave and out of my shell
and keep a close watch on what and what not to tell*

*I am not so sensitive when someone asks me
about any feelings or actions that prompt me
It is usually their interpretation that perplexes me
Yet I do my best to take it responsibly*

*However, I do regret it until I get a next chance
Until then mind and head play the unbearable dance
Feeling sorry for the hurt I caused
So very easily for the words that I tossed
I wish I had my feelings just paused!*

*So I am sorry again and again
how do I recover or regain?
extending my humble apology again and again
to strengthen the bond and overcome the pain*

Second Chance
1 September 2013

I understand if you wish not to respond
Here after I won't bother you or correspond

Just scribbled a few words, few lines
to shorten the gap with some words and rhymes

In the process of erasing unpleasant memories
and rewriting moments with pleasant stories!

Like a child I wish I could forget, dust and move on
Why as adults do we cling, nag, brag or even drag on

For reasons obvious
or even mysterious
A child grows to become an adult
but an adult wishing to be a child
seems just so ridiculous
or is that just miraculous

As a child I learnt and accepted life so easily
But as an adult neither could I accept nor understood
relationships, affection, feelings or love so readily
is/was it because children are overly protected?

Through karate and self-defence
I fight my mind as if in a pretence
I rattle and learn to handle self-criticism
Keep sanity and to maintain my optimism

Splashes of Pink in My Life

Can there be a re-connection for a second chance?
Or would you prefer giving me the radio silence?

There were so many sorries that you had said
I accepted them and they put a smile on me instead
The only sorry that I said, I am truly sorry as I said
I feel you are just as soft, genuine, and precious
If the feeling is mutual, please respond ... am curious

I understand if you wish not to respond
Wondering if at all you will correspond

Wish you all the very best
Sorry for being such a pest!

Leftover
26 August 2013

The very thing that I desire in life,
Feels sharp like a throat with a pointed knife

For the very reason I avoid intimacy
walking away (from relationships) I found was easy

I am not asking you to marry me
neither am I asking you to carry me

If you wish to spend some quality time with me
And let the flow of things decide what is meant to be

Splashes of Pink in My Life

Jai Ho! The National Treasure
6 June 2013

Faster, smarter and certified!
In you there is nothing to be rectified!

Only slow and gradually getting to know you
Slow and steady is how you like to proceed too.

You say you are an open book
Waiting to get to know you and life's outlook
For your glances and emails am on the look

If I send you this poem, this text
Makes me wonder what will you say next?

On me you have this kool minty effect
and when I dig deep it is a sublime reflect
From saying too much, I have to hold myself back
else how will the mystery and chemistry stack?

Did I tell you am good at massage for the foot and back?

I desire to increase our intensity and connection
the greater the retention stronger is our foundation
Is this how you feel too ... a two way feeling?
Or am I just in a fairy tale story dreaming?
Without asking, I wish you are more revealing!

I wish to spend lots of quality time with you
Getting undivided attention and devoted time with you
I am here and pursuing my own dream far away from you

Time with you is like a happy intoxication
Obviously wanting more without any hesitation
Afraid you are becoming my new addiction
Once addicted, I don't want to leave and go into rehabilitation
Silently praying that this infatuation
converts to a life long eternal admiration!

Why does my heart long to be with you
Why does the girly mind yearn to be with you
I wish I could get rid of my mind and its possessions
Because it is too much to handle its crazy obsessions
Mind and heart always on a constant retaliation
Mind keeps asking,'what next, what next?' on a constant repetition

Why in you do I long for a true friend, love or even a companion
Is this what will make me feel a real accomplisher or even a champion?

So I finally quit ... and walk away ... no more to pursue you and me
Don't like the uncertainty ... or even being a ginger eating monkey
I walk away to free and relieve my mind
From the whimsical fantasy in which I bind

As a girl this unexplainable feeling, the thought of you is so nice
Cool, clam and under control with your feelings like mint and ice

The monthly cycle and the hormones makes yours truly super agitated
No emails, no phone calls, nor chat initiations makes me very irritated
Before I burn myself, I call it quit
in the fire in the heart that I have lit

Am sorry if this made you feel sad, bad or even hurt you
I have no choice but need to rescue my crazy mind too
Sometimes being light hearted is the best thing to do
I guess this comes very naturally for you!

Splashes of Pink in My Life

When I run behind and demand attention & affection
It has only made the affection run away in defraction
Late but sure I realised it is to be withdrawn within me
Things will happen and unfold if it is meant to be

Feels like I am walking on a tight rope ... taking a risk
I feel attached to you ... too soon too quick
so gambling my mind and heart, as if to frisk

Would I regret this one day?
Or could this be a turning point too?
Only time will have to say!?
If at all ... what will be your next move?

Jaise Koi
December 2012

Jaise koiii
Jaise koi khoyi huee cheeze
Mil jaye to bahut hai azeeez
Kya waqt kare kamaal
nahin kar paye khud ko sambhaal
Sune sirf dil ki dhadkan
mile jab dono ke tan badan

Behak gaya tha munn
na tha koi shabdh
dhuk dhuk bani zubaan
ankhon ne sametaa chehara ka muskaan

Issi yaadon ko liye hum
pal do pal khushise jiye hum
Na samaj paye zindagi ka raftar
Kya yahin hai pyaar ka ek puraskaar

Kya jeepayengey ek doosrey ke bin
Kaun jaaney katengey aise kitney din

Am I Independent?
April 2013

I am not independent
I am but very much in dependent

I depend on the air that I breath
I depend on the air and its cool breeze

I depend on the food that I eat
I depend on the heart and soul to meet

I depend on the life force energy
I depend on nothing but me

I depend on the love and yearning
I depend on food and earning

I depend on my motivations
I depend on life and its creations

I depend on nobility
I depend on humility

I depend on new creativity
I depend on my potential and its ability

I depend on everything around me
I depend on nothing that is beyond me

I depend on my surroundings and me
My surroundings, do they depend on me?

I depend on my quest for life
I depend on my zest for life
I depend on it for the rest of my life

I am not independent
I am only in dependent

I depend on thee
for you to see the true me

So am I really independent?
I am very much dependent!

I Have No Choice… But Patience is Bitter
April 2013

I have no choice but to wait
I have to catch a fish and I have put the bait

When will I meet my soul mate?
I feel this game, is it destiny or fate?

What is it that I have on my plate?
And what should I do and at what rate?

I am still waiting to be approached for a date
Will it be boring or will it get late?
For my soul mate to open my heart's gate?

How long, how long do I wait?
For the fish to catch my bait?

Eternal Love ... True Love?
April 2013

Why do I set myself so high?
With expectations from where I can not fly!
Instead I have a great fall,
Not in love but with disappointment above all!

It is so easy to wander off in fantasy and imagination...
When reality hits, ecstasy diminishes and dawns realisation!

Is this the nature of a girly mind,
Or is this love that people truly find?

If there exists true love that people find,
I wish that to be in all relationship in which I bind!

Splashes of Pink in My Life

Reinventing How to Fish
March 2013

I wait, wait and just have to wait
for a good fish to catch the bait

I need to keep my mind ticking, keeping it occupied and busy
else the silly mind wanders away, obsessed and crazy

I wonder if I cross your mind and make you smile
when running, working or even just for a while

Let the man do the running and chasing
if he is real, interested or even worth embracing

Keep your cool and carry on ladies
and just be pretty and look like fairies

It is your charm and confidence that strikes his chord
Until he is ready, do not rush, hurry the concord!

Ahh, all the above is too easy said than actually done
Carving my cravings into such poems for sheer fun!

Thank you for making me feel this way, the way I feel and do
Bringing life to my poems making it absolutely so real and true

The other half, the remaining half
March 2013

Neither do I want to be bound by any obligation
Nor do I want to rush into things out of frustration
Nor do I want to set any great expectation
Nor do I want to give any explanation
Is this one big fat confusion?
I feel like a cat on the wall
Not jumping as I am afraid of the fall
Do I keep walking or just keep watching
Sitting on the fence, my brains I keep scratching!
If I jump, it may be a huge risk and end with a thump
If I run, I may slip, fall, over accelerated be overly done!
If I sit tight, I will be doing nothing but lips to bite
I wish to follow my dreams and pursue without any doubt or plight
I want to complete my PhD as I value higher education
Eventually become a lecturer and strengthen my foundation
I believe in enjoying life yet being simplistic
Yes, I want to pampered and be very romantic
I seek a companion who has a sense of humour
Who communicates well and has courage and valour
Someone who will make me light and make me laugh
Someone who is intense yet can joke and chaff
This is my dream this is for my best half!

Splashes of Pink in My Life

Overcoming Boundaries of the Mind
December 2012

*Repetitions, habits, and unpleasant patterns in life
that keep me emotionally bound and mind constantly at strife*

*I realise, it is the mind that creates the boundaries
I realise, it is the ego that digs and in itself buries*

*In a hurry to get out of the rubble
With effort and might we struggle
quickly drawing further down like that in quick sand
Wanting to get out and hoping for that helping hand*

*When you realise it was none other than self inflict
there is laughter and hardly any confusion or conflict
When this realisation dawns like that under the bodhi tree
It gives me direction, logical steps, actions needed to set me free*

*In order to know the beginning
the mind wanders and when finally comes to an ending
it dawns upon me the beginning was the very first ending
and now that very ending has become a new beginning*

*Vedanta says wake up and shake up
Thou are that in any direction down or up!*

*When you transcend all limitations and boundaries
You abide in the eternal peace without any hostilities*

*In a desperacy to get rid of the desperateness
I travelled hither thither and only through awareness
Was I able to overcome the task at hand
STAR is the key and that's the only way to LAND
STAR is the Situation Task Action and Results*

In a State of Confusion
October 2012

The Western way - emotional connection before physical intimacy
The Eastern way - physical privacy prior to mental connectivity
I see neither one right nor the other wrong
Why the mind undecided and takes so long
Show me the way, give me the courage to walk my path
Procrastination and unhappiness - symptoms are of the aftermath

I have given up even before I tried
Wasting my time and people's brain I have fried
I don't want to do the things I feel I am going to fail
As a result, without preparation I just get out and bail
Why does mind appear so dull and is on a constant batter
Wake up and realise ... everything I have is on the platter

I want to just lay back, relax and do nothing
How do I escape what appears to be so loathing
Only through poems I express and explode
Yet the things to do remains a huge load
Is there a person who will be a confidant, a companion
inspite of my quirkiness and strange thoughts and opinion

Self-conscious, I project what appears to be pleasant
Yet feel true growth is in the places that are unpleasant
When I meet people for the first time
I set boundaries worth only a dime
When I meet the acquaintances again and again
Creating expectations and setting up myself for pain

Splashes of Pink in My Life

I feel the great one to one connection
When I lose myself, I am afraid of rejection
Is it because I am only seeking and wanting attention
Wondering how am I perceived and how is my projection
Am I aware and why am I seeking constant validation?

At times this feels like a second chance to life
Everything on the platter, yet why the mind at strife?
In hope & desire to move forward and give my best to strive

Experience on the Ice
October 2012

Where did my spirit go?
I feel I am going too slow
Hoping my experiences will help me flow

Ice skating after 14 years
thought it would be easy and no fears!
Thought it would be easy to pick up and slide
Kind of like driving, swimming, just wear the shoes and glide
When on ice ... it was so difficult to balance
mind and body absolutely tense and imbalance
Fears creep in the mind like I was carrying a very heavy load
Am I am like a frog living in my own world, like that arrogant toad

As I glided I realised my fears
Pressure from my mind and its peers
When I realised the fears then it was also the shoes
And as I glided the shoes started becoming loose
As I fell I was able to let go
When I swapped the right shoe
After the 15 minutes training and demo
The balance came back to sow

When you held my hand
It felt like a magic band
When I felt your well toned muscle
Wanted to have fun and wrestle

At the end of the night
Mind and body felt so light
Had Bhopa Devi by the cool moon light

Splashes of Pink in My Life

Lights glittering on the Docklands Waters
Lot of fun, beautiful smiles and laughters

After dinner I gave you a butterscotch 'toffee'
Instead you invited me for a drink, for a 'coffee'
My mind was fluctuating but why did it hark?
Was it me or was it you who constantly felt the spark
In denial and in confusion I felt a bit safe to escape
Uncertain and yet certain I went back to my cave
On one had, I was very flattered but felt the invitation was a bit too fast
Does physical intimacy bring two people close and has its own spell to cast?

I wondered if things were going to go any further?
In wonderment, I wrote this poem as a self-reminder!

Do not chase, run, possess or even go after
So called love as it slips away quicker and faster
Let nature take its time to blossom and to rafter

Bhagwaan se ek Guzaarish, ek kwaaish
October 2012

I do not understand this feeling this emotion
Unable to digest, find a logic behind such notion
Where only unspoken feelings remain
I wish I could dissect or describe this pain
Where logic does not reach
Where silent tears only screech
Unable to pacify my mind, heart or soul
Am I the only one or have I dug myself into a hole?
How do I get out of this, or persuade me to cajole?
Why do I have such high self expectations?
I feel like a failure when I do not meet my reputations
Though failure is a stepping stone to success
Work load and things I have carried in EXCESS
Self inflicted, self created ... have I got myself trapped?
Situation like a silk worm ... in a cocoon completely wrapped!

Get me out of here
Get me out and set me clear!
Don't walk away, just glance or even leer!
I hope nobody feels like this, Oh Dear!

In Response to a Poem
October 2012

Kal ki batein kal mein reheno do
Aaj ki batein abhi mein beheno do
Zindagi mein muskurake chalte raho
Kissiki shikayat kabhi bhi na karo
Taqdir ko taarif mein badalte raho
Zindagi ke kisson se behadh seekhte raho!

Emotional Intelligence
October 2012

I guard my feelings so tight
In tightness I become so plight

Am I the one to lose my will and might
In shear madness, do I flee, freeze or fight?

I pour out my heart and soul
Into the work and start to roll
Before my feelings take its toll

Am I being insensitive to others feelings
When unmentioned and walk away from such dealings

The heat of the passion feels so temporary
Might as well enjoy what lasts perpetually

The wise ones say, enjoy it … but don't quite believe it!

How do I feel when I see a loving husband
and a beautiful wife by his side?
How do I feel when their kids play in the beach and sand?
With a warm heart at life and its situations with a smile I abide

A poem dedicated for life and its inspirations
To those who have driven me to such sensations
Giving meaning to life with multitude dimensions

Life inward is about intentions
Life outward is about perceptions
A balance between the two is quotient of emotions

Fishing the Mind
August 2012

He says he is an open book
Will I get a chance to turn the pages and have a good look?

Felt the butterflies in my tummy
His deep masculine voice ... warm and sunny

Messages and calls that I missed
Was like catching bubbles that fizzed

The mind getting dejected and disappointed
Ways I found to pacify and entertain the mind instead

Felt like a uselessly hopeless feeling
Is this magic or is there logic to instinct and believing?

One side saying, "You know what? Just forget it!"
The other saying, "You know what? Go GET IT!"

In confusion ... tearing the sides apart
In this poem, I express, articulate and craft

Will fate bring us together?
Is it worth the wait, or should I not even bother!?

Balancing work and life is surely an intellectual thing
Balancing mind and soul is the cause and effect of everything!

Das Leben
August 2012

Oberflecke oder tief ist das Leben?
Was hat mann zu das Leben gegeben?

Was gibt zu nehmen?
Was gibt zu geben?

Das Leben ist nicht langweilig
Und auch nicht zu schwierig

Geniessen und nicht vergessen
Bleib in heute und nicht schwanken!

Eine kleine Stueck by Jaishree Ravindran

Bits and Pieces
December 2011

Desperateness makes a person appear unattractive
Smartness makes a person surely very attractive
Elegance is very charismatic
Reverence that is so just automatic
Innocence makes one believe
Intelligence makes one relieve
Attraction to intelligence
is smartness to innocence!
Attraction to smartness
is innocence of the intelligence!

mix of east and west can be a sweat ...
mix of east and west can also be a waste ....
choose what you want to taste
or choose it and let it fit you for the best :)
East or west ... Jai (with all pun and humility) is the best

Am merely a reflection
I am ... You are ....
are just mirror reflection
thank you for your great inspiration
in spirit we find lot of good rations
perhaps that's why it is called inspiration!
Hearty congratulations
For the reader, enjoyer and the wider nation!

Vesting in Time
December 2011

Life is a waist of time
Waste is the life of time
To have the time of your life
Need to shake off your waste
Dance away and move your waist
let things not accumulate on your waist
else the body accumulates a lot of weight
once accumulated, it becomes difficult to wait
endless effort to remove all that collected waste!

Splashes of Pink in My Life

Space Realisation
July 2011

That which can not be measured is not Maya
That which can be measured is ever changing
That which can not be measured is reality
That which can be measured is never permanent!

The space between two places is distance
The space between two events is time
When the two combine begins a journey
Make the progress a special tourney

The space between You and me is a relation
The space between God and me is self-realisation

Hari Smaran
July 2011

Hurry and Worry make a man dis-eased
Hari aur Vari make a person ... ah soo pleased

Hari naam hee dawaa hai
Hari kaam hee lajawaab hai
Hurry mein Hari bolo
Worry mein bhi Hari bolo

Sanskrit mein Vari hai rich in gifts
Sanskrit mein Vari ko kehtein hai ek river
Hari gives peace of mind and itself uplifts
Hari who is abundant love and infinite giver

In Hari I rest in life's Vari
In Hari I have no worry

So Hari and Vari make a person at ease.

Splashes of Pink in My Life

Lost in Your Eyes
April 2011

*Your eyes so deep
Unfathomable like the sleep*

*Your eyes so deep
a reflection unspoken I keep*

*Breathless have I become
To the unconditional love I succumb*

*Is this surrender?
Strength that I render*

*Neither defend nor offend
blending is the way to mend*

*Go with the flow
Like the light and its glow*

*So supple and tender I feel
Is this life and its ultimate Zeal?*

I am Alright
January 2010

Sleepless and tired in restlessness
Was I always in deep bitterness
I only feared and often shook in jiterriness
Felt as if I was always in the darkness
Lonely, and silently - I screamed and screamed
Grinding my teeth as I deemed
Oh my oh my
Oh why oh why
why did this happen to me?
often the answers I couldn't see
Is this what life had to be?
and still the answers I couldn't see!
Twitching, tossing and turning
Biting my lips and running
helpless was I feeling
for all the pain that was causing
repeatedly was I asking
Oh why is this happening to me?
I should have known what type of person is he!
Was it really love?
Was it because of the vow
was it longing for emotional security
or was it life's mere cruelty
Always taking the blame
blames only turned into a large flame
no longer could the fire be to tame
For I just wanted to run and hide
but at the same time doubted and wondered
How do I leave everything aside?
No longer sat I and pondered

Splashes of Pink in My Life

I cared for nothing but my security
and also my life, my prosperity
Now I see the light
Even in darkness and at night
the incident has given me will and might
to have a clear vision and sight
Let the lessons and experiences be
a caution and warning for those who see
that life is too precious
allow nobody to be ferocious
No longer am I now stiff at night
hope these words have given you an insight
over is the bitterness and the fight
but please be assured am (going to be) alright!

C'est la Vie
Jan 2009

Life is what we make it to be
Sweet sour salty or simply tasty
What was I waiting for?
Looking farther no more!
The waiting game is now over
Waiting makes the fruit appear sour
I don't know what is in store for tomorrow
Being in the present moment, there is no sorrow

Picking and cleaning rubbish
makes one realise
what is being lazy and sluggish
and time just flies

am laughing out of loss of breath
is this love and happiness at its maximum depth?

A sense of feeling lost yet kept
expansion of self - wide and breadth

Splashes of Pink in My Life

Kaalam Maarie Pochu
Amudha Ravindran, August 2009

Amma samaiththa unavai
Anbudan ettru saappitta kaalam pochu

Adhigarathudan, thevai-illa-unavai
Alavillamal vunnum kaalam aachu :`- (

Idupai chuttri erandu tyre peruthuppochu
Nadakkah udal moochi mutti sorrndhu pochu

Thulli gudhiththu thuru-thuru-vena vilaiyadiya kaalam pochu
Thuvandu vizhundhu TV parkkum kaalam aachu

A Poem by Mommy (it's in tamil) - for Youngsters of the present world!

Waiting for You
22 November 2018

It is nice to wait when you are coming home to me
It is nice to know when you are home waiting for me

I look forward to waking up early in the morning
I look forward to breakfast and the day as it is dawning

I anticipate your long morning hugs
I reciprocate with warm loving snugs

I feel safe secure and very loved in your arms
Uff the way you hold me and dance in your charms

I enjoy spoiling you with my culinary delight
Please to watch you as you relish every bite

I look forward to our conversations and stories over food
I look forward to your teasing, wild imaginations, they are so good

Thank you for the amazing pink flowers
Magical feelings behind those delicious flowers

As you sleep, I admire your pink rosy lips
Secretively admiring your curled eyelashes' tips!

Splashes of Pink in My Life

Dear Cristian

A heartfelt thank you for everything!
You have inspired me to write this poem ☺

Waiting for you....

It is nice to know someone at home is waiting for you
It is nice to wait when someone is coming home to you

I look forward to waking up in the morning
I look forward to breakfast & the day as it is dawning

I anticipate your long morning hugs
I reciprocate with warm loving snugs

I feel safe, secure and very loved in your arms
Uff.... the way you hold me and dance in your charms

I enjoy spoiling you with my culinary delight
Pleasure to watch you as you relish every bite

I look forward to our conversations & stories over food
I look forward to your teasing, wild imaginations, they are so good!

Thank you for the amazing pink flowers
Magical feelings behind these delicious flowers

As you sleep, I admire your pink rosy lips
Secretively admiring your curled eyelashes' tips

A poem by Jaishree Ravindran
With love — Jaishree 22-11-2018

A Poem for Cristian by Jaishree

As our last chapter closes, what were the pearls of wisdom that you were able to capture from this book?

1. What did you get out of this book?

   _____

   _____

   _____

   _____

   _____

2. What came to your heart, mind, and body as you read this book?

   _____

   _____

   _____

   _____

3. What resonated with you most from this book?

_____

_____

_____

_____

_____

4. What would you like to share from this book?

_____

_____

_____

_____

_____

_____

Collection of Poems

5. What is your take home message from this book?

_____

_____

_____

_____

_____

The Games We Played As Kids

Help-Help

Number of members to play the game – in odd number

Even numbers (including the Den)

For example, 11 members + 1 Den = 12 players

Instructions

The den is a person who catches people. The den runs out to catch people who are single. When the den is running or coming to get you, you scream for help: "Help-Help". If you are out, i.e., caught by the den you become the new den. If you have a person with you, the den cannot make you OUT.

Alterations to the game: the den runs out to catch people and the instead of 2, the runners to form a group of three or more people (a nominated number, e.g. 3 4, etc.) to get immunity for the group.

Lessons from the game:

- Awareness
- Surrender
- Asking for help when required
- Run as fast as you can
- Dodging the den
- Go to rescue someone
- Let go if there are 3 people... doing this in a skillful and tactful manner else all of them become out.

Lock & Key
(Also known as Medicine & Poison)

The den catches people running. The person being caught can either sit down and say 'LOCK' to get immunity form the catcher/den. The LOCKED person is released from the LOCK position when another team member goes out and touches them by saying KEY.

The aim of the game for the den/catcher is to get all in the LOCK position.

Lesson for the team members is to help others with a key and revive when a team member is LOCKed out.

Note the words:

LOCK can be replaced with POISON

KEY can be replaced with MEDICINE

NB: Outdoor game... can be played indoors in small groups.

Lion & the Mouse

All players form a large circle.

The game begins with a nominated lion and a nominated mouse (can be more than one).

The team members forming the circle are to protect the mouse from the lion.

The aim of the game for the lion is to get the mouse and for the mouse to run away from the lion

There are several tactics; the lion can be skillfully let into the circle while the mouse is let out of the circle.

Lessons:

The lion and the mouse can be seen as the mind and the ego... sometimes inwards, and sometimes outwards.

Lessons learnt:

- Team co-operation
- Alertness of the mouse
- Skillful lion
- Learning to use and move the boundaries
- Have fun

Chain Reaction

The den catches a person from a group running around. The den and the person caught hold hands to create a chain to catch the rest of the people. As one person is caught a chain is formed. Only people at the end of the chain can tag the other people 'Out' to join the Chain.

Lessons

Once you become out ... give your full co-operation to your chain. Make the chain strong. If a person is tagged/caught when the chain is broken, this is not acceptable.

Needle and Thread (also known as Intercept)

One den and many others.

The den is running to catch someone (can be anyone) and if someone intercepts by crossing the path, the person intercepting becomes the new path for the den.

The den goes to catch A, when B intercepts the path, the den then aims to catch B. The den can alter the path to catch anyone prior to an intercept.

Lagori – Seven Layers of Existence

A small ball is used.

There are two teams. The team that destroys the layered and stacked stones sets it back again.

The team that breaks the layers restacks without becoming OUT with the small ball hit by the other team.

One Team (Team A) is breaking and once the layers are broken, the other Team (Team B) gets the ball. Team A runs and restacks LAGORI without getting OUT. Team B uses the ball to hit Team A OUT.

This can be an outdoor/indoor game.

Seven Up

All players sit in a big circle. Start saying 1, 2, 3, 4, 5, and 6 in the direction of the person indicated by their hand.

Left hand crossing over to right shoulder means the person sitting to their right to say the next number.

Keep playing until number 6. For 7, the person says '7-UP' with their hand on the head. The direction pointing the game to continue restarting from 1.

Lessons from the game

- Awareness
- Body, mind co-ordination

Om Game

All players sit in a circle.

Numbers that are multiple of 3 and numbers ending in 3 are to be said as OM

E.g. 1, 2, OM, 4, 5, OM, 7, 8, OM, 10, 11, OM, OM, 14, Om ... etc

Whose Line is it Anyway?

A question is raised, and the next person says the question without answering as a statement - question to be answered with a question.

Can be played as a group where one member steps to answer the question.

Do not repeat the same question.

For example:

- Person 1 – So where do you want to go?
- Person 2 – What do you think?
- Person 3 – Can you see where is the game going?
- Person 4 – Do you still want to play?
- Person 5 – What is happening here?
- Person 6 – Am I in the zoo?

Creation and Innovations - Renovating Ideas

An object will be given to each team and they can come up with creative ideas to use it (limited time). The team with most ideas gets points.

For example: A hat

Examples of creative ideas:

- Fashion statement
- Use it as a bowl for chunky soup
- A begging bowl, etc.

Guess Who is it?

Two teams to play: Team X and Team Y.

Team X decides a celebrity, a book or a song.

The other team questions - Team Y to ask questions (10 questions). And Team X can only answer Yes or No

Bonus Points if answered within the first 5 questions.

Guess Where am I and Who am I?

Two people seated/standing – one behind the other. The person in the front ties their hand in the back and uses the hands of the person at the back.

The person in the front verbally communicates with the den. The person at the back interlocks their hands and communicates using their hands with the den. All hand gestures and body language communications is through the person at the back.

Based on the communication (verbal and body language) with the den, the is audience to guess what the situation or scenario of the communication is.

Lesson from the game:

- Learning body language

London London Statue (also known as FREEZE)

The den is facing with their back to the team and says out loud 'London London Statue' prior to turning around. The team members freeze to a statue. When the den is not looking, the members can change their statue or position or posture.

The aim of the game is to make the statue smile or move without touching.

If a member hits the den, then all the team members are to run beyond the boundary to save themselves from becoming OUT.

Lessons from the game:

- Awareness
- Everything changes
- Present moment is inevitable
- Make others laugh or smile
- Melt others with your joke, acting, etc and get out of being a den

Recommended Books

These are some of the books that I have thoroughly enjoyed and highly recommend:

1. *Think Like a Monk* by Jay Shetty
2. *Celebrating Life* by Rishi Nityapragya
3. *Help Me* by Marianne Powers
4. *Rising Strong* by Brené Brown
5. *Braving the Wilderness* by Brené Brown
6. *Never Split the Difference* by Chris Voss
7. *State of Affairs* by Esther Perel
8. *Life Above Zero* by Lauren Kerr
9. *138 Dates* by Rebekah Campbell
10. *Lovelands* by Debra Campbell
11. *Essentialism* by Greg McKeown
12. *Five Love Languages* by Gary Chapman
13. *Why Men Don't Listen, and Women Can't read maps* by Allan and Barbara Pease
14. *Make Every Man Want You* by Marie Forleo
15. *Why Men Want Sex and Women Need Love*
16. *Get the Guy* by Matthew Hussey
17. *Atlas of the Heart* by Brené Brown
18. *Karma* by Sadhguru Jaggi Vasudev

19. *The Code of the Extraordinary Mind* by Vishen Lakhiani
20. *Captivate* by Vanessa Van Edwards
21. *The Way of Integrity* by Martha Beck
22. *Flow* by Mihaly Csikszentmihalyi
23. *The Secret of the Red Crystals* by Sujatha Sharma
24. *Atomic Habits* by James Clear

Acknowledgements

I would like to acknowledge my parents for their unconditional love and support. My maternal and paternal grandparents – Jeji Avva, Hello Thatha; Yassoda Avva and DK Thatha. My brother Anand for his continuous inspirations and my spiritual teachers in infinite forms – past, present, and emerging.

And YOU, my reader!

I also want to acknowledge all those who encouraged, believed, and supported me in silence and in speech.

A big shout out to Natasa, Stu, and the Ultimate 48 Hour Author team who helped make this dream a reality!

With humble gratitude, infinite love, and respect
Jaishree Ravindran

About the Author

Ever since she started reading memoirs, Jaishree wanted to write a book and share her knowledge and wisdom with the world.

She believes that when knowledge is shared and applied, the wisdom multiplies. She has a passion for innovative cooking, where she is known for being given random ingredients and coming up with something unique and delicious.

As a global traveller and someone who has lived in five countries, Jaishree loves to discuss self-development and is curious about how the mind works.

Her first book, *Splashes of Pink in my Life* is a collection of wisdom, stories, hints and tips about life, cooking and self-development.

As her quench for applied knowledge never ceases, she is currently pursuing a PhD in the field of lactoferrin.

Jaishree Ravindran

Jaishree Ravindran is the author of Splashes of Pink in my Life. An engaging and down-to-earth speaker, Jaishree shares the accumulated knowledge and wisdom she has gained through life experience, self-development, and deep reflection.

Jaishree is a firm believer that knowledge is best when shared and applied as it leads to a collective wisdom multiplying among communities.

As she is blessed with many talents and passions beyond her professional career, Jaishree shares these topics with her audiences and is now undertaking a PhD in Lactoferrin. She holds Bachelor of Technology in Food Technology and Master of Dairy Science and Technology.

Through her many travel experiences, Jaishree's Indian cultural origin and love for adding value to people's lives has developed into practical and engaging topics that her audiences really enjoy diving into.

Jaishree's energy and zest for life and learning can be felt in her speaking and presentation style as she easily connects with people from all walks of life. She has a unique ability to serve her audiences by helping them get them into a deep reflective mode of learning about themselves in a way they have not considered before.

Jaishree can create a custom presentation depending on your audiences' needs, yet her signature talks are:

1. Innovative Indian Soul Food

- How to cook Indian food that tantalises your taste buds
- Delicious and easy recipes that can be done fast
- Step-by-step hacks on mixing Indian dishes and spices

2. The Seven Study Strategies for Success

- The 7 principles to successful studying
- The magic plan to effective studies
- Keys to the application of your education

3. How to Create Your New Career Roadmap

- Unpacking your vision for your future career
- Networking strategies for fast-tracked success
- Unlocking hidden opportunities for career succession

Photographer: 'aarjifotografi'

Contact Details:

Jaishree.SplashesofPink@gmail.com   +61 477 419 271

www.ingramcontent.com/pod-product-compliance
Lightning Source LLC
Chambersburg PA
CBHW030036100526
44590CB00011B/228